Advance Praise for
Own Your Opportunities

"Juliet will always bring light to your day. It's a nice read when someone else can express your thoughts better than you can yourself."

—**George Wallace**, Comedian/Actor

"Through magnetic storytelling, Juliet masterfully shares truth serum for your workplace toolkit. In a pertinent and poignant reveal, she frames the need-to-know reality that survival in the workplace requires more than oxygen. *Inhale.*"

—**Patricia Russell-McCloud, Esq.**, International Motivational Speaker and Bestselling Author of *A Is for Attitude*

"*Own Your Opportunities* is an important read for any leader who is trapped in a workplace culture of marginalization. Leaders—women or men—who have the capability, capacity, and confidence that is unrecognized and/or intentionally underutilized will find wise advice and affirming assurance to seek windows offering new visions and paths charting new directions for their professional and personal lives."

—**Martha P. Farmer**, Founding Director of Leadership America (Leadership Women™)

"At one of her lowest career moments, Juliet heard the voice of God commanding her to write. I'm so grateful she listened. By sharing her story of achievement and disappointment in corporate America, she has laid out a path to career and personal freedom. This is the good news gospel of knowing your strengths, naming your dreams, and seizing your space in this world that we all need right now."

—**Nia-Malika Henderson**, Senior Political Analyst at CNN

"Juliet Hall shares her journey of learning more about what self-regulation looks like when creating our own opportunities for success! Her details of how we can improve self-cultivating strategies are inspiring, and she provides motivating tools as a part of self-discovery for personal and professional growth."

—**Wendy Eley Jackson**, Lecturer at University of California
Santa Barbara

"I remember the day Juliet told me that she couldn't wait for me to 'own my opportunities.' I had just spent an hour telling her about how directionless and unfulfilled I felt. Honestly, the last thing I wanted to hear was that I needed to take ownership of my own life. What I wanted was for Juliet to console me and tell me everything was going to be alright but that's just not Juliet. She doesn't settle for pleasantries or mediocrity, and after reading her book you'll know why. *Own Your Opportunities* taught me to never make myself small to make others feel good. I walked away understanding that the gifts I have been uniquely given are important and that the world absolutely needs my gifts just as much as I do! If you are looking for advice or need a mentor in your life, I recommend reading *Own Your Opportunities* as a great place to start!"

—**Brit Suits**, Mentee of Juliet Hall

"Wow! Juliet eloquently inspires all of us to remember our gifts in the midst of our triumphs, challenges, and disappointments. Her storytelling is riveting as she illuminates her faith and personal journey of self-discovery and self-maximization. Juliet enables the reader a unique and compelling opportunity to look through the window of a Black woman's experience in corporate America. And in a time where companies are focused on building inclusive cultures where all employees can thrive, this book is timely. *Own Your Opportunities* is an outstanding read, and Juliet's inclusion of a roadmap and strategies to true success in career and life is a gift that will keep on giving."

—**Fran Dillard**, Vice President and Chief Diversity Officer
at Fortune 500 Company

"COVID-19 ushered in a mass exodus from the workforce that has become known as the 'Great Resignation.' Workers around the world continue to explore their career options and life choices. While we hear a lot about the worker shortages and the economic effects of this trend, the conversation has shifted to acknowledge that people aren't necessarily quitting, instead they are pivoting. Juliet manifested her 'Great Pivot' a few years before the pandemic-inspired masses and vividly shares her hard-won insights in her book *Own Your Opportunities*. Juliet artfully tells a personal story that is honest, vulnerable, and authentic while imparting practical advice for anyone looking to own their unique opportunities. This book also provides a glimpse into the not-so-glamourous realities that many women and African-Americans experience in corporate cultures. It is a great read for anyone interested in learning more about micro-aggressions and the impact they can have on employee engagement. *Own Your Opportunities* is a great book to give to professionals at all levels who may be considering a career transition, those who have made transitions already, and leaders who desire to learn more about what motivates top performers before it's too late."

—**Ebony Howell,** Atlanta-based Human Resources Executive at
Fortune 100 Company

"I found two significant benefits from this book as a reader. The first benefit was as a professional striving to have a purpose-filled career centered on nurturing and using my gifts. The second benefit was as male ally in a leadership position striving to support professional women achieve excellence in corporate America. Juliet, in her own unique and authentic voice, delivers on these two benefits in this page-turning book as she shares insights on her path toward achieving excellence in her journey. She gives examples of challenges, including multiple leadership support failures, to understand and support her career path as an African-American woman. She also highlighted how, despite the environmental challenges she faced in the workplace and the trials and tribulations of life, she was destined to further hone in on her gifts and use them for the better of those around her. It's a story bound to make you reflect and inspire where you are on your personal journey, while challenging you as a leader to create a better work environment for all."

—**DeWayne Griffin**, Fortune 50 Executive and Board Member

OWN
YOUR
OPPORTUNITIES

OWN
YOUR
OPPORTUNITIES

A STORY OF
SELF-DISCOVERY AND
SELF-DETERMINATION

Juliet
HALL

Post Hill
PRESS

A POST HILL PRESS BOOK

Own Your Opportunities:
A Story of Self-Discovery and Self-Determination
© 2022 by Juliet Hall
All Rights Reserved

ISBN: 978-1-63758-540-5
ISBN (eBook): 978-1-63758-541-2

Cover design by Tiffani Shea
Interior design and composition by Greg Johnson, Textbook Perfect

Post Hill Press
New York • Nashville
posthillpress.com

Published in the United States of America
1 2 3 4 5 6 7 8 9 10

*I dedicate this book
to every woman and girl
who dreams.*

Contents

Prologue

And I just sat there, reflecting, in my car where the world was still. I had just left my meeting with Heath and waited for the lump to form in my throat because, well, that was what I thought I was supposed to do—cry. But there was nothing there, nothing to be found.

Just emptiness.

The likelihood of your dreams doesn't exist here. Heath's words swirled in my head. *You're articulate and well-spoken, but you're not humble. You assume more autonomy than your role allows... you struggle with relationships...you're not a team player.* Heath then quoted words from a fable about what an ideal team player looked like, which, according to him, didn't describe me.

But I had remained calm, even as the walls closed in on me in that meeting room, while Heath made his closing arguments. We never worked on anything together and never served on the same team. He was simply the mouthpiece for the case that had been building on me. I knew my time had been coming to an end; I had already prepared for it. Leaving, amicably, was the only path for my sanity, dignity, and chance to find dream fulfillment on my own.

Both Heath and I settled that my last day would be on September 15th, just a few months away, to finish and transition my current work that could be completed from home. Oddly enough, it would also be my anniversary date. How poetic that the day of my ending shared the date of my beginning. And now, another new chapter was upon me.

The final box was checked.

Everything, and I meant *everything*, had gone according to plan.

I was free. And yet, freedom had never felt so strange. There was no one to control, mute, or block me anymore. But still, there I was, clutching the steering wheel in my parked car, stalled, as if I either didn't want to leave or was unsure if I could. It was like being one of Pavlov's dogs in a behavioral conditioning experiment.

An old familiar ache crept inside me. I removed my oval company badge from my knitted fuchsia suit jacket and cradled it in my hand for the last time, reminiscing, as light beamed off the plastic. For so long, the badge represented much of my identity. My thumb brushed across my name and years of service on the badge, and as I sighed, the lump inside my throat I had been looking for suddenly began to form.

"What now?" I broke my own silence, staring into space. The Georgia summer sun beat through the windows. I turned the ignition and blasted the coolest setting of my air conditioning. And then, an unexpected response struck me.

Write.

It was an automatic, inaudible response, yet a firm whisper that raised the tiny hairs on my arms and snapped my body to attention. I recognized the voice, too. The same unspoken clarity had shined on me months ago, in early February, which foretold my company exit.

There are many labels for the internal consciousness we all have. Some call it gut. Others call it intuition. To me, it was the voice of my Creator. And that voice gave me only one instruction.

Just write.

But then the nightmares started.

My head became a haunted house.

The faces were a blur, their bodies more like silhouettes trapped in a gray fog. I heard the familiar sound of voices, people I had worked alongside for many years. Human shadows huddled before me, and as I moved about, I heard them whisper, "She has a nice smile, but she doesn't fit in here." Then, I saw images, like mystic holograms, passing me and through me, as if I didn't exist. And finally, there was a rushing sound, a giant roar that yelled, *"Get out!"*

The nightmares wore on me like a crown of thorns. I often woke up in tears in the middle of the night, shrieking. "God!" I cried, curled in my bed, cupping my ears. "Make it stop! Make the voices stop!"

I told no one about the dreams, too afraid to be written off as either weak or dramatic. Trauma had drilled into my psyche like the constant jabbing of an icepick, breaking me apart until I seriously considered if all the negative things said about me were true.

"Why couldn't they just *accept* me?" I shouted into the air, trying to make sense of my rejection, while streams of water dripped from my face. My mouth tasted coppery, like I was swallowing pennies. *Yes*, I was direct and strong-minded, articulate, not afraid to challenge or speak my truth to power, *and* I was supportive, loyal, and a good soldier who got results—all the things a leader should be.

Betrayal and bitterness grew over me like kudzu. I sank deeper into my covers. "God, finish the work you started in me!" My body was wracked with desperate sobs as I fought to break through this dark invasion and find the light within myself. "Use my voice and the gift you gave me!"

I remained cradled in my bed, even as layers of amber broke through an indigo sky. Some days, I didn't leave the bed at all.

CHAPTER 1

Recognize When You've Outgrown a Situation

Unapologetically, I touted my knitted fuchsia St. John suit and Stuart Weitzman heels, dressed and ready for the showdown. A classic string of pearls adorned my neck and gave me that final touch of ladylike elegance. My natural, pressed hair radiated a silky straight gloss, the edges smooth, a non-negotiable for African-American women in ultra-conservative organizations. At forty-one, my honey-bronzed face still held the smooth firmness of a woman much younger. Surprisingly, there were no lines or etches of battle wounds from years of working in a corporate system that was neither created by me nor for me.

My heart raced as fast as the milliseconds on a stopwatch. It was time for me to head to work and beat the Atlanta traffic, but I stood frozen in front of my bedroom wall mirror. The expectations from people I cherished mounted heavily on my shoulders.

Juu-u-lie! My ears perked to the slow-cracked drawl of my late paternal grandmother, Mattie Mae, and the memory of her unfiltered, crass tongue that made you laugh one minute and cussed you out the next.

Mattie Mae hailed from Rock Hill, South Carolina, born just a few years before the Great Depression, when jobs were as scarce as food on the table. She dropped out of fifth grade to assume the only job she ever knew for women who looked like her—a domestic servant. She wasn't just "the help." She was the "top chef" of her day. With her black gnarled hands, she cooked royal spreads and cleaned for White families well into her mid-seventies to sustain herself and pour into me and my older sister, Annette, the best way she could.

I reflected on how she never missed an opportunity every Easter to dress us up like Barbie dolls and pair us with Easter baskets before showing us off to the old ladies at New Mount Olivet AME Zion Church. We weren't just her "chaps," we were her hope and her dream. Annette became a doctor, and I, a corporate manager. We "made it" in her eyes and became her kinsman redeemer of sorts—making up in her life for everything that went wrong.

Don't you lose dat good job, nah...ye hear! I could still see Mattie Mae scolding me with her hands dented into her fatty hips. My eyes watered as I remembered her.

Oh, dear. Another voice shifted its way into my memory. It was the soft eloquence of my maternal grandmother, Ethel Mae, whose words now waved over me like a flag as I continued facing the mirror in pensive silence. She, too, was born in the Depression era. Raised by a sharecropper in Mountville, South Carolina, she was a farm girl-turned-sophisticate who refused to be confined by the blunt dictates to Black women of her time. She was a career woman who mastered dual professions as an educator—she taught language arts in middle school and English classes in college—and as a radio broadcaster. Grandma Ethel's life was a series of checked boxes and accomplished goals. The hallway in her house was a walk through a shrine. One side boasted an infinite display of plaques and awards, including her honorary doctorate and induction into the SC Broadcaster's Hall of Fame. The other side showcased her pride in her children, all nine of them. And they all went to college, a household commandment.

Ju-li-et, Grandma Ethel continued, evenly enunciating every syllable in one melodious swoop like a broadcaster...or an English teacher. *You're smart. You will do well, whatever you decide to put your mind to. But you have got to control your mouth!*

My mind swirled with other voices, too.

Girl—keep your head down, don't rock the boat. Just do what they tell you to do. Your job is to make your boss look good! My living African-American mentors, mostly baby boomers raised during the Civil Rights era, often advised me to keep me out of trouble, as if I were a slave in the early 1800s.

And yet even now, in 2016, after eight years with a Black president in the White House—and a woman on the verge of becoming the next one—it was painful to realize some corporations still didn't value diversity, equity, and inclusion. Sure, many companies *hired* for diversity. But if you were a minority and wanted to survive, you learned to *assimilate*—look like, think like, and act like those at the top who determined your worth.

And so, for two decades, most of my work life felt like a tap dance, though I dreamed of ballet.

You make that good money...don't be a fool, those sage voices added as their final warning, lingering in my head.

My body swelled with one final deep breath. I gazed into my own chocolate eyes in front of the mirror until my rapid heartbeat slowed its pace.

"You got this, Juliet," I convinced myself. Regardless of my own pep talk, sweat still beaded my forehead with the imminent uncertainty of my professional future.

It was risky not having a clear roadmap of what I would do if I left corporate America. As a child of the seventies, I didn't see many examples of people switching careers and I didn't want to appear unstable, like a college student with an undeclared major. You chose a profession that paid the bills and stuck with it, like my mom, who was a career music teacher, and my dad, a career blue-collar service worker. Loving your work was only a bonus.

That was the rule. But Grandma Ethel was an exception. She lived life with so much fluid freedom, and it inspired me. I needed her strength right now. My stomach roiled as if I were standing on the edge of a cliff.

"God, help me," I uttered, as I finally stepped away from the mirror and proceeded to my garage, where my silver Lexus sedan awaited. I whipped out my iPhone to activate my playlist before departing my home, a remodeled four-bedroom, Victorian-inspired house in the green suburbs of Northwest Atlanta.

I found solace in the strong, high-octave vibrato of Tamela Mann that transcended my aching soul to the very feet of God. I filled my car with this song each weekday morning to stabilize my blood pressure while I drove to the office, a glassy multistoried building that now seemed more like a cage.

For forty-five minutes, I clutched the steering wheel and zipped through unusually loose traffic on the Atlanta beltway. It was summer's eve in the Peach State. The sun flexed its rays early on this warm June morning. But I welcomed this southern heat over the scorching trial that awaited me at nine o'clock about my career—a meeting to "be on the same page."

For the past year and a half, my corporate career, which at one time offered me so much opportunity, had transformed me into a sitting duck. And so I needed strength on *this* particular day, more than ever, because, well...today was the day.

The day of final reckoning. The day where things would either change for the better or for the worse. The day, I thought, where some human with a high office, one who didn't know my story, held the power to render a judgment that could interrupt my professional plans, delete my generous salary, and wipe away my existence from a company I'd dedicated years of my life to help grow. It could all happen in the blink of an eye.

"Everything has an expiration date," I groaned.

At 8:50 a.m. or so, I arrived at the corporate complex and marched through the office toward the human resources section of the building. Faceless coworkers along the hallway, who wandered and chatted outside a break room after fixing their morning coffee, saw me approaching and cleared my path like the parting of the Red Sea.

Did they know something I didn't? Their heads were down, no eyes peered at me. There were no disingenuous "good mornings," "hellos," or "how are you today?" questions that typically greeted me every morning. Perhaps because only two types of people really existed in human resources—those on their way in, and those on their way out.

I massaged my chest as it throbbed harder with every step toward the meeting room. I stopped at the door, wiped my sweaty palms on my skirt, and took one final long breath before turning the knob. Two people sat at a rectangular table in a room that screamed, "This is where the bad news goes down!"

A small, sterile conference room with dreary gray walls and no windows appeared as hopeless as playing tennis on a rainy day. Long white lightbulbs emanated a low dull hum. A steel conference table with several empty chairs seemed haunted with the ghosts of past firings, disciplinary improvement meetings, and organizational restructurings. I couldn't help but feel as though I were a suspect awaiting questioning on an episode of *Law & Order*.

A late-fiftyish, silvery-haired senior manager from human resources, Heath Pulski, sat on the left side of the head table, while his assistant sat on the other side at the far end. Heath averted his eyes but somehow managed to acknowledge my entrance with a nod and awkward motion to have a seat near him, as if I were truly in the power seat.

My eyes narrowed at his silk polo shirt and khaki trousers. He was more appropriately dressed for a day on the greens than for a formal face-to-face with another seasoned leader in the company. He didn't notice my disapproval and it didn't matter. His good-ole-boy status wasn't going anywhere.

With ease, I took my seat, relaxed my arms on the chair, and flashed my million-dollar smile at Heath as if I had just earned immunity on *The Biggest Loser*. Acting was everything. As a leader, I had to show strength in the face of opposition, even if I was scared as hell.

So, there we were—I, Juliet, good ole boy Heath, and his mousy administrative assistant, who never raised her head above her laptop. One thing for certain: It's never good when it's just you and human resources in the room.

"Nice suit." Heath spoke in an even, tenor voice that could easily mimic a male Siri.

"Mmm." I acknowledged his comment with a quick nod.

His icebreaker was as terse as the immediate discourse that followed. "You're well-spoken...and direct." Heath glanced

quickly at his notes. "Yet you intimidate people. You struggle with relationships on your team. They feel uncomfortable
around you."

I briefly looked away from him, sighing, to hide my frustration at why my being articulate and to the point was both a
surprise *and* a problem for others. I'd never heard a Caucasian
woman or man be criticized for being well-spoken or for not
mincing words. Heath didn't lead with my work performance,
only the perceptions and feelings that other people had of me
and my communication style.

And I knew who the culprit was—Connor Rumpkin, a ten-
ured group leader with the company.

Connor, or "Con," as he liked to be called, was a wrinkly elder
who sat in the same seat, and in the same role, for many years.
His leadership style was anything but collaborative—more old-
school and hierarchical, reminiscent of a boot camp sergeant.
But he was a close pal of the senior vice president in the company, which helped him more in his career than his personality
or ability to inspire people.

Eighteen months ago, a job opportunity was posted inside
the company to lead a new business unit that involved corporate
training and storytelling. I was selected to build and manage the
team, which afforded me a stage. It was the perfect marriage of
utilizing my natural gifts of public speaking to teach and share
the story of a brand I loved, and I drank the Kool-Aid.

The problem was, though, I was *too* good at it. My gifts had
blossomed like a velvet rose. I reveled in the finality of discover-
ing who I truly was—an inspirational voice that could empower
people.

I was getting booked to speak on large stages and share tips
on career development, women's empowerment, and leadership

to diverse audiences, sometimes on behalf of the company and other times unrelated to the company on my personal time. Encouraging people from a stage made me feel like a genius. It was where I belonged, where the world made sense to me.

One of my biggest highs was speaking to an audience of 1,500 people in a college commencement ceremony, a tremendous honor for which people of high renown and influence get tapped. My reputation as an inspiring, captivating voice began to precede me from that moment on, and before I knew it, the streets were promoting me.

My confidence soared like a peacock parading its vibrant feathers, which raised some eyebrows and made some people in the building, including Con, think, "Who does she think she is?"

Meeting with Con was a chore. I always had to get prayed up before our one-on-ones.

"I want you to limit your external involvement." Con got right to the point. It was our first quarter meeting, and he called me in to set new expectations for my role. "No more speeches, talks, or board engagement. I want your focus to be all internal now. I have projects I need you to do."

As Con rolled out my new job description, an acute sickening, aching feeling of loss washed over me. I was like a baby yanked away from its mother.

"But, Con, this is my sweet spot!" I pleaded, leaning forward on the edge of my seat. Desperate, I tried to remain calm and swallowed hard to dissolve the lump forming in my throat, straining to get the next words out of me. "This is how I add value, what I was selected for, how I connect. Didn't you say you wanted to give me more work in my sweet spot?"

Con did not budge. His eyes were like two metallic gray holes. I caught a glimpse into his soul and discovered nothing there.

I added, "Well, then, why can't I speak on my own time? At church? At colleges, speaking to students about their careers? I love serving people in this way!"

"You are an agent of this company, you spent most of your career here," he said, chuckling, "What else could *you* possibly have to speak about?"

Heat swelled inside my body, and for a few seconds, all I saw was red.

"Jobs change," he continued, looking down, shuffling his papers. "If you still want yours, then focus on the projects I give you."

Troublemaker or threat, which had I become? I clenched my fists. "Why are my speaking engagements a problem? It doesn't conflict with the work I currently do. I'm doing good things, making an impact. Don't you want me to grow and be better?" *Or stay in my place*, I wondered. "I mean, what's the real issue here?"

"Look." Con's words were slow and intentional. He scanned messages on his iPhone like that was more important than his time with me. "I'm not trying to hide you."

With pursed lips, I tilted my head and raised an eyebrow, unconvinced.

"But you are *not* the spokesperson for this company," he scoffed, as if the very idea was ridiculous.

Dejected, I wanted to retreat to my office, but our meeting hadn't ended. Deep inside, I knew God didn't create me to be contained and mentally shackled. I also knew this company—and Con—had the authority to dictate whatever they desired because the truth was, I chose to work there. If I wanted to stay on the payroll, I would have to soldier up and obey. Period.

Con paused, put his iPhone down, and looked back at me. I could see his mind thinking before he slammed the gavel. "And, Juliet, Georgia is an 'at-will' state. It's up to you."

And that was that.

Then Heath cleared his throat, breaking my reverie about Con, and brought me back to the present to continue his contrived narrative of my "performance" issues.

"You're a great public speaker," Heath continued in his matter-of-fact, bulleted script, "but you're not humble. You're trying to build a brand, on the cover of a magazine. You didn't get approval for that. You assume more autonomy than your role allows. You post pictures on social media, trying to promote yourself."

True, I had posted new headshots, radio interviews, and pictures of speaking engagements on my personal social media. The magazine cover was only to promote the storytelling work the company had assigned me to do. Perhaps it appeared as though I had become an emerging celebrity—a brown-faced female leader standing out in a company where there were no women of color in the C-suite. It clearly turned heads.

People must have been buzzing inside the office, "How is *she* getting all these opportunities?"

How, they'd asked?

I just shook my head.

Because I never waited on handouts. Because I always saw myself as bigger than my role. And instead of playing the race card, whining about being overlooked for a promotion, or waiting on my supervisors to develop or "sponsor" me, I learned to be my own champion and started owning my opportunities.

That was how!

And yet, still, the room got smaller and darker with the rude awakening that my initiative and success were essentially acts of treason. The pretty Black woman with the wide-toothed smile was not a mindless puppet, and she believed she was capable of more. But I got too big for my britches, pushing the boundaries of my sandbox and getting my hand slapped as a result.

They want to determine what success looks like for me, I reckoned. I fought to keep my face stiff, though deep inside I brewed with righteous indignation. They didn't see me as a leader, only a glorified contributor with limits in their kingdom.

My body heat crept up like a volcano on the brink of eruption. My chest tightened at the thought of these good ole White boys asserting boundaries for me, a forty-one-year-old African-American woman, on what I was allowed to do, or *not* do.

I saw Heath glance over at his secretary, trying to catch her eye, perhaps to make sure she was capturing all the notes or for reassurance that he was on track with the script. He was in his stride and closing in on the kill.

With his quick and robotic voice, he continued, "You have three options. You can stay in your current role, but you'll be put on a performance improvement plan. You can move to another team. Or, you can leave, with our support."

The drumroll stopped. The volcano inside me stilled. The knots in my stomach from earlier that morning dissipated. No more mystery, no more uncertainty. In that moment, my standing with this company became as clear as the June-blue sky.

I froze, contemplating the crossroads I now faced. Heath made no reference to my breaking any policy nor doing something performance related to work—it was all about my communication style and, perhaps, the growing publicity that the company, or Con, did not support. Instead of bowing my head, saying "Yes, sir," and kissing the ring, I stood on the brink of being let go.

There was a risk to spotlights. It made you a target.

Stay. Transfer. Or, leave.

"If you stay," Heath interrupted my thoughts, "you will be put on a performance improvement plan—and, uh well, things are already not working for you in your current department." I knew what he meant. I would eventually get fired.

"But, Heath, these are all the things I've done for this company," I defended myself.

I gave him the highlights of my corporate track record—my work in previous departments, my leadership in the community, my mentoring other women and representing the company in international leadership missions—all value-added impacts. Scores of written letters, honors, and verbal accolades from other peers and leaders commending my work, leadership, and even *teamwork* all seemed to be forgotten at that moment.

"You've made some positive contributions to the company."

Some? Really.

"But our culture is non-confrontational. That's our fault. You have struggled with relationships on other teams." There was finality in Heath's tone. This issue was not up for debate.

I had been labeled "passionate, confident, strong, independent"—qualities often celebrated in men but code for "hard to get along with others" when applied to me. It's a double-edged sword being a voice, to not be afraid to speak out, to challenge or hold others accountable. People either loved you or hated you for it.

And transferring to a different department was a sentence to be ignored and overlooked—an invitation to become the company's cautionary tale. That was no option either, at least not for me.

This was not a meeting to "be on the same page." This was a meeting to transition me out of the company peacefully, amicably, without creating a bunch of noise.

Checkmate.

I couldn't move. I stopped breathing. There was no one I could call to defend me or rescue me. I had poured years of my soul believing in a company that didn't believe in me.

I just closed my eyes and dropped my head, knowing I had no option even though Heath had presented me with three.

He gave me a moment to digest the gravity, if not finality, of the situation, before asking me, "Juliet, what is your dream job?"

My dream job? What a curious, perhaps intrusive question at that awkward moment, words I never thought would have escaped Heath's lips. Dreams inspired freedom and hope, a stream of possibilities—opposite to the corporate culture of control which Heath proudly patrolled.

Yes, I thought, I knew what my dreams were. Deep down, I always knew. They breathed in me, constantly floated in my thoughts like visual whispers from God. A spokesperson, a voice that lifted humanity and brought the best out of people—those were my dreams. I'd always loved a stage, whether it was acting out a character or standing behind a podium.

I lifted my head, and with conviction I declared my impossible dream. "My dream, Heath? I want to be a face and corporate spokesperson for this company, an ambassador of sorts. I want to one day be teed up and considered for that role." I did not stutter, did not blink my eyes.

Heath paused, glanced at his notes for a second to allow my dream to be heard. "Well, the likelihood of that dream doesn't exist for you here."

And just like that, he put the nail in the coffin. It was final. My dreams didn't belong inside this company.

"But," Heath quickly added, "we want to help you achieve your dreams. We want to offer you..."

A golden opportunity, I thought, so we can all move the hell on, amicably, without the clamor that a well-spoken, intelligent woman of color could potentially bring.

Yet still, from that point on, every word he spoke became muffled and garbled.

My mind flashed images of my professional life and all the good I thought I did. But the ceiling was set firmly for me with no thought of my ascending above their line. I had been reduced to their labels, and they didn't want me anymore.

How did I get here? What did I do wrong? I had nagged God with those prayers for the past eighteen months with tears running down my face. I sat in the chair in that conference room asking myself those same questions now.

I looked down with pinched eyelids, reflecting, as my body filled with regret. Perhaps I should have bowed down, lowered my eyes, and quietly stayed in my box. The company certainly paid me enough. But then, I couldn't be what *I* wanted to be, and my spirit waned like the crescent moon until there was little power left in me.

My arms grew heavy having to constantly hold up a mirror, examining myself closely for flaws and second-guessing myself, as I morphed into considering the opinions of the patriarchs— and its female allies—regarding me to be more valid than my own. The more they paid me, the harder it was for me to leave— until the last eighteen months, when I dared to believe I could be more than what this company wanted me to be.

"How does this all sound to you, Juliet?" Heath broke my chain of thoughts, to make sure I was listening, or perhaps as an invitation to contribute ideas on my imminent exit.

"Huh?" I said, clearing my throat. I straightened my back in the chair.

Did he just roll his eyes?

"I'm sorry. Come again?"

Heath went through his spiel once again. As I listened this time, the chip on my shoulder began to slowly diminish. I eased back in my chair, imagining the possibilities of building a larger stage of influence for myself without the limits enforced by the company.

And suddenly, it was as if the June sun powered its rays through those dreary gray walls. A window opened in my soul. I saw a path to freedom, a chance to finally *be*.

Hell, why should I be an unfulfilled laborer in someone else's kingdom when I could create my own? A small smile hinted on my face as my mind lit with ideas.

The shrill click of a turning lock echoed in my thoughts. The cage door slowly opened. My heart fluttered with both anticipation and anxiety, but yet, my body stalled.

Was this really happening?

Heat emerged in me once more, as an invisible voice in my head whispered that I had broken no policy nor did anything reckless or grievous to deserve this judgment. My eyes hardened with anger. My hands balled into fists. *Don't let them win*, it said. *Don't walk away from your money and benefits. No...make them fire you, then fight and make them pay!*

Uh-uh, baby girl. Don't be a fool! A chorus of whispers in my other ear interrupted. The emphatic voices from my African-American mentors chimed in urgent unison once more. *Swallow your pride, you hear? You gave them your best...now, go! And take what's on the table!*

Mattie Mae and Ethel Mae were probably rolling over in their graves.

Heath leaned in, his assistant ceased her furious clicking on her laptop and for once shifted her timid eyes to me, and they both held their breath, waiting for me to say something. The atmosphere in the room was charged with anticipation, like riding up the crackling incline of a steep rollercoaster.

I relaxed my hands and placed them on the table. I held my head high, locked my eyes into Heath's and spoke the outrageous words I presumed he wanted to hear.

"Thank you, Heath," I said softly with a smile. "I'll leave."

CHAPTER 2

Start Somewhere

The year was 1996. Spring was in full swing, bursting with vibrant hues and the homecoming of cheerful chirping sounding from the trees. The emergence of the "information superhighway," or the internet, was baptizing the world. More and more people were getting acclimated to a new way of gathering information, adjusting to the dissonant static and shrill sounds of dial-up.

Meanwhile, Atlanta had just recovered from its version of "Black Woodstock," known as "Freaknik." Waves of Black college students from across the nation flooded the city to enjoy a weekend of "free love" in bumper-to-bumper traffic on I-85 and downtown streets. A parade of vehicles thumping bass moved in stop-and-go fashion. Young men and women danced and drank along the roads, on top of cars, and in parking lots the entire weekend. The pungent wisps of burned pine and skunk-like notes puffed throughout the air. There was not a White person in sight.

Once the noise of Freaknik ended, the city resumed its planning for an even bigger party—the Games of the XXVI Olympiad. But while the energy in Atlanta brimmed with exhilaration at the countdown of hosting the Summer Olympic Games, I was a frantic twenty-one-year-old senior at Spelman College scrambling to come up with a post-graduation plan that didn't involve returning home to Columbia, South Carolina.

Graduation was less than sixty days away. The fresh spring air buzzed with anticipation on the green, hallowed grounds of America's oldest private historically Black liberal arts college for women. Already, I felt the pride and nostalgia of ending my four-year chapter with the nationally recognized institution I called home. "Spelman, thy name we praise," the sacred words from the hymn, were forever etched in my heart, translated into a duty for me to live up to the college's legacy of women who change the world.

Pressure mounted as classmates began to talk about next steps—medical school, law school, a master's degree program somewhere, a fabulous new job, and/or marriage. I was happy for their success, but with each excited squeal of good news, my stress level increased because I was still trying to figure it all out for myself. I knew for a fact I wasn't going back home. I had not bothered to apply to graduate school, and my college sweetheart and I were nowhere near talks of marriage. I was convinced that leaving college without a job offer from a reputable company would make me a failure.

Afraid, I drummed up imaginations of not living up to the expectations of those who knew me as a high school standout. I reigned at the top of my high school class, was voted by my classmates as class speaker, served as editor-in-chief of my high school paper, got accepted into the SC Governor's School for the Arts, won a ton of speaking awards, and simply excelled at practically everything I did—except high school softball. Thick envelopes with my name printed on them stacked the mailbox from different colleges and universities wanting me to apply.

"You can apply to any school you want, but you're going to Spelman." Like thunderous gray clouds looming across the sky, my mother's words blocked the light that beamed hope and possibility into my ambitious heart. I had considered academic institutions known for journalism, such as Northwestern University, and worked hard as a student to position myself to have options. Yet, the freedom I thirsted for at that moment was a mirage. Spelman College didn't even have a journalism or communications major, but that didn't matter to my mother. In fact, none of my desires seemed to matter. "I want you to go to a Black school for women."

Freedom. Well, that's what I wanted. The freedom to choose, the freedom to laugh. The freedom to even understand why fluttering warm impulses ballooned inside my depths at the thought of a teenage crush. While many of my classmates dated or frolicked with friends on the weekend, I stayed isolated at home, where there wasn't much laughter. I wasn't even allowed to enjoy much television except for the news, a weeknight mandate at six o'clock sharp.

I learned to find escapes through reading books and writing. I lost myself in stories that ushered me to a different world where I could live freely as a teenager and imagine a different life.

When I finally met freedom at Spelman, little did I know that Momma's decree would become a blessing in disguise. Across the street shined an array of Black brilliance, the men of Morehouse College. Who knew that Atlanta would be the land flowing with milk and honey? Starry-eyed, I became a kid at a candy store, thinking, *I'll try one of you...and you...and most definitely you!*

I determined to make up for all the fun I missed in high school. In time, though, I drifted, not knowing how to responsibly handle my freedom. Distraction cursed my childhood dream of becoming the person I watched every night on the news. I destined myself to be a public figure like Tom Brokaw or Jane Pauley. But I attended one too many parties, skipped a few classes, lost my college scholarship, missed out on opportunities to apply for summer internships with TV networks, and before I knew it, it was time to graduate. The driven, focused high school valedictorian lost her way, barely maintaining a 3.0 GPA.

And here I was, a nervous wreck, panting and sweating profusely in search of a job. I signed up for several interviews with investment banks at the career office in Upper Manley, the student center on campus. Being rejected for job after job made me regretful for not managing my college years better.

But nothing prepared me for my interview with the last bank standing. It was not an investment bank but rather a regionally known retail bank that had a management training program—a leadership pipeline—that guaranteed an entry level supervisory role within the bank upon completion of the training.

Game face on, I was ready-set-go for my interview. The usual questions of "Tell me about yourself, what are your strengths and weaknesses, how would others describe you, and tell me about a time or experience when...?" were all questions I could now answer with authority.

I stepped into the interview room, a basic square office with shiitake brown paint, just big enough for two chairs and a desk to separate me and my interviewer, the assistant vice president of the retail bank based in the smoky tobacco lands of North

Carolina. A White man in his late forties, he was the poster figure of a conservative banker, sporting a tailored dark gray suit and silk crimson tie. A simple gold band wrapped snugly around his left ring finger. His face seemed a little blotchy, though, as if he had gotten wasted the night before and was dehydrated.

Three minutes into the interview, I detected something other than my answers that preoccupied the banker's interest and glowing eyes. A hard blush grazed through me, reminiscent of a time I was thick into my middle school puberty when insolent seventh-grade boys gawked and poked at my oversized breasts.

"Sir? Wait—is there something wrong? Something on my suit?" I tilted my head downwards, then shot a fiery glare into his reddening face.

The banker shrunk with guilt, like a child who got his hands caught in the cookie jar.

Heat crept up the back of my neck with growing indignation. "Because, um, I notice you keep looking at it!"

I didn't want to pick a fight, but I had to check him. I needed this job—it was my last hope—but at that moment I wanted to pluck out his lusty eyes. Sure, I was a curvy chick with a small waist. But I showed no cleavage in my navy suit. My jacket was forgiving enough to subdue the pronouncement of my generous upper endowment and not make my big girls scream, "Get a load of me!"

"No, um, there's nothing there." The banker mumbled under his breath with slight remorse. His face flushed a red so deep it almost matched his tie. He cleared his throat with a slight cough, head lowered.

From that point on, I managed to continue my interview as if the incident never happened, while his eyes reformed and steadied upwards on me.

I got the job!

Now, I could breathe again. I had someplace to go after graduating from college and could support myself with the $29,000 starting salary the bank offered.

The company moved me to Winston-Salem, North Carolina for my training, where I sat in a cubicle on one of the top floors of a medium high-rise building that boasted bright, endless views of the small emerald city.

I was big-time!

Three months flew. Upon graduating from the bank's management training program, I screamed with the news that I would be returning to Atlanta despite my being assigned to a second shift operation. Working a second shift didn't sound very sexy, but I wasn't really a morning person anyway. I would take any assignment to get back to "Hot-lanta" and be among other people of color.

But my world came to a screeching halt when I drove into the parking lot of my first supervisory assignment just minutes outside downtown Atlanta. This was not the modern high-rise building with big windows and picturesque city views that, for three months, framed my work-life in Winston-Salem.

Instead, I got out my car and gaped at a tired, two-story red brick building with few windows that prophesized drab walls, fake art, and an overall soul-sucking atmosphere on the inside. With eyes growing in horror, I glanced across the street and gasped at one of Atlanta's well-known strip clubs, allegedly owned by the mafia on Piedmont Avenue, sitting there, just a few blocks away from the MARTA Lindbergh Center Train Station.

"What the...?" I mouthed, aghast.

I clutched my purse and looked both ways as I walked across the parking lot and into the railed doors of the bank's operation center. When I was escorted to my assigned department, I almost fainted at the optic in front of me. It was if I were starting my new career from the bottom all over again—literally, in a basement!

I didn't realize such an environment was even possible during the training I received in Winston-Salem, which was very polished and "corporate," but clearly nothing more than an illusion. I was trained in a calm, squeaky-clean, sparkling office environment with a dress code in mind—suits, skirts, stockings, dress jackets, and low heels.

"You don't need to wear that here. We dress business casual," my new boss, Jed Tucker, senior manager of Check Encoding Operations, stated abruptly and matter-of-factly.

It was my first day meeting him, and my desire to make a strong initial impression on the man who would control my pay increases immediately fell flat. He scoffed at my black Kasper suit with dismissive eyes as if to say, "That dress for success thing doesn't apply here."

Jed was a heavyset man with bushy blond hair, shoelace lips, and glassy eyes. He looked sloppy in his baggy khakis, due to his towering height and a belly so big it sloped over his belt buckle.

As he gave me the nickel-and-dime tour of the underground kingdom of which he was so proud, he stopped every ten steps to point his chunky fingers and bark orders to the other supervisors on the floor.

"And by the way, this is Juliet. She's new...out of the training program." Like an afterthought, that was my introduction by Jed to my new peers, the four other supervisors in the department, who each gave me a quick, single shake of the hands, then hurried off and away from Jed's presence.

Surprisingly, Jed's heavy frame zipped throughout the murky floor in the basement department. Dust flew everywhere. Paper clips sprayed the carpet. Four stations of heavy machinery, encoding devices with image technology, dominated the center floor and blasted a constant roar.

I noticed a random huddle of chatting employees leaning against an out-of-service machine, who parted like the Red Sea whenever Jed shot a questioning look their way.

The worker bees were called IPs for "item processors." Many of them were African-American women in their thirties, forties, and fifties, who had glazed looks in their eyes. Several wore headphones or earplugs, either to give them some pep or to cancel out the noise from the bustling machines. Either way, they immersed themselves in their own worlds, kept their heads down, and focused on their monotonous, individual production like a glorified assembly line.

"My God, my God...why hast thou forsaken me?" I mumbled under my breath, stunned, knowing that the obnoxious hum from the machines would overwhelm any sound emitted from my mouth.

After ten minutes on the tour, it didn't take long for the light to dim in my own eyes. My neck involuntarily lowered, as if someone had slapped a chain around it. My feet throbbed from walking in heels. The powder that hung in the air from the constant flow of innumerable checks and deposit slips streaked all over my black Kasper suit. My wide-toothed smile disappeared and my heart sank as if someone had lied to me.

After the tour, Jed guided me through a brief hallway of offices just outside the main floor. I was glad to finally get to a still, muted space, even though my head still rang with the clamor of buzzing machines.

He nonchalantly introduced me to his secretary, Aisha (pronounced I-E-sha), whose desk we had to pass to get to his office—though he more like looked past her, as he continued to gloat like an emperor with his head up, chest out, and arms swaying like trees with a breeze in the park.

Aisha was probably in her mid-forties, with short-cropped hair and a dark brown oily face scattered with sun spots and moles.

"*Oh!*" she said with raised brows and widened eyes when she saw me.

I knew exactly what that meant. She had never seen a Black woman in a supervisory role in Jed's department before.

"Nice to meet you, Aisha," I said to her, as she scanned me up and down and nodded her head with approval.

"Welcome...glad to meet *you!*" Aisha's smile followed me into Jed's office.

So, there we were, my new boss and I, sitting in his office that contained standard block furniture and enough space to comfortably fit four or five other chairs for a small group meeting. A vintage lamp and wood-framed picture of Jed and his wife adorned his desk. A wide desk calendar stretched beside his DOS-operated IBM computer, which resembled the shape of a square box and took up the entire right side of the desk. A tall wooden bookshelf stood perpendicular to the matching wooden desk, used mostly for office accoutrements rather than for holding actual books. Contrary to the hectic production floor, Jed's office was clean, orderly, and calm.

But *I* wasn't calm. My nerves still rattled from the calamity of the enclosed environment. It wasn't just the thought of working in a bulky, cluttered department that vexed me. It went much deeper. A weight descended on my spirit. An invisible burden loomed in the air, which reflected in the lifeless expression on the workers' faces. This haunting reality, I determined, was an omen.

I sat across from Jed, who perked up as he proudly explained how he was known for meeting his production deadlines while staying within budget. That was his claim to fame, his halo effect.

"Deadlines have to be met by eleven every night, otherwise it delays the bank's posting schedule," he said emphatically. That was mostly the spiel—meeting deadlines by any means necessary, so that customer transactions could be posted to the accounts on time.

Jed also explained the organizational structure and gave me a briefing on the other supervisors I would be working with in his department, all of whom I had already met on his zipline tour. He offered very little description about the other supervisors other than to reiterate their names and how long they had worked there, which wasn't very long—four years or less.

He didn't know too much about his people, it seemed.

And then he dropped a bomb.

"I *will* yell at you." Jed's face was straight, and the words came out of nowhere.

Suddenly, everything stopped.

My mind was at a loss for words, as the taste in my mouth grew rancid. My heart pounded in fear. I just sat there, gulping, imagining this towering figure speaking harshly at me.

Was this normal?

"Got any questions?"

I shook my head, holding my breath, and dared not leave my seat without his permission.

"Great! Glad to have you. See you tomorrow morning. Come around eleven o'clock."

And with a nod, Jed released me to go home.

"What's going on? Why are we backed up with checks?" Jed barked at me one day. A few of the IPs within earshot jumped, shot questioning looks my way, then buried their heads in their work to avoid eye contact with him.

"We're short five processors today," I informed Jed. "They called out. One of the machines is down, and maintenance is checking on it." Out-of-service machines were a big deal, as it created bottlenecks in the operation, potentially impacting deadline performance. People also called out every day, I'm sure to convalesce from the furious daily race of meeting deadlines, or from Jed's incessant fussing and cussing.

"Get some people down here! *Now!* Check other departments to see if people want some extra hours!" His fingers pointed furiously in the air. "And stay on top of the IPs and keep them working! Some of them are moving too slow!" Jed stomped in the direction of the broken machine to check on its status, triggering a light cloud of paper dust flurrying at his heels.

"Sure," I said, rolling my eyes at his back.

This was the norm, the daily grind, that I endured for almost two years now.

Work was a daily battle, listening to Jed yell and humiliate people, then later make up for his "assholery" by inviting some of the supervisors to the strip club next door for a drink after work. That was his only attempt at team bonding.

Depression slowly rooted in me. Sunday evenings became a sad love song. Dread coiled in my chest like a snake whenever I pulled into the parking lot of the dungeon, and mild tension headaches clung to me almost every day. I began smoking cigarettes in the closet to relax, though that didn't last long. I was afraid it would darken my teeth and make my lips turn black. And it wasn't cute either, at least not on me.

It was painful experiencing Jed leave a wake of demoralized supervisors and processors behind him, including me. He especially liked to pick on Eddie, another supervisor in the department and one of my peer buddies.

Eddie was a fresh fair face with green eyes and thick brown hair. A clean-cut, preppy type, he was a diehard University of Georgia Bulldog graduate. We were the youngest supervisors on the floor and very close in age. The other ones were much older, so it was no surprise that we naturally gravitated toward each other.

Jed toyed with Eddie a lot, often calling him "stud man" because he came to work crisply dressed. He was charming, had swag, and no trouble getting endless dates with women.

Eddie and I often commiserated with each other during the long evening work hours when Jed wasn't around to harass us.

"I'm not staying here," he confided. "I'm just getting a few years of management experience before going to grad school to get my MBA. I'm already looking at some programs."

"What! Really?" I stumbled to find the right words, hoping my shock would mask my disappointment. "That's great, Eddie. Wow!" I wanted to be happy for him, at the fact that he was in control of his endgame. Instead, my eyes stared blankly at the floor as I realized I didn't have a game plan of my own. My body trembled at the thought of being left alone with Jed in the dungeon.

He gently nudged my left arm. "Figure out what *you* want to do. Then do it." Eddie made it sound so easy. "Just do it," he said again.

I didn't grow up in privilege like Eddie, who drove an old Porsche that his father gifted him when he graduated from the University of Georgia. Our circumstances were different. I had to stand on my own two feet and carry my own water.

Within a few months, Eddie left. He got accepted into an MBA program at a respected university in Texas, and I never saw him again.

With my work buddy gone, the processors that reported to him now reported to me. I aspired to bring fresh air into the department and did so through building relationships with my new team. Those were actions I could control.

Some of the processors went to college, some didn't. Even though the job wasn't glamorous, they took pride in their work and brought a level of dignity to it—showing up on time, keeping their workstations clean, and keeping a keen eye on their encoding to avoid money posting to the wrong account.

Several nights I rolled up my sleeves and worked alongside the processors to learn their stories—their families, education, and goals. Pretty soon, I developed good relationships with them, and we became like family.

They were no longer processors to me after that point; they were people—with blood, tears, hopes, and dreams.

And we had fun, while meeting our deadlines, celebrating birthdays, baby showers, or milestones. I would order food for them if we had unusually late nights. I labored to boost morale through recognition, incentives, or just plain talking to them. I wanted to lead through inspiration, unlike Jed, who led through intimidation. Even the Black women who initially thought I was *high-falutin'* came around and got to like me, eventually.

One of the people on my team, Frankie, a beautiful, light-brown, stylish woman in her forties with critical eyes that noticed everything, sat with me in my office sometimes to talk, albeit briefly. She told me her story about overcoming a rough divorce with her abusive ex-husband and her desire to go back to school.

"You can do it, Frankie. There's nothing stopping you. It's never too late." I could see the light grow in her eyes as she began to see her future self. "You're incredibly smart, grounded, and focused. You pay attention to quality. You're the best at that on our team, you know?"

Frankie grew a few inches taller sitting in her chair, while I marveled at the transformative effect of dreams. She glamorously swung her lustrous shoulder-length hair like she was riding on top of a car in a parade, all because she saw herself in a winning space. I'd never seen her smile so brightly, and my heart melted even more.

Then, she shifted the conversation to me.

"What about you, Juliet? What do you want to do?" Frankie leaned forward, smiling at me like we were sisters.

I toyed with my pen, reflecting on her question. My dreams were personal, hidden in the most inner part of me, where my heart beat the strongest.

"Come on, you gotta tell me," Frankie said, nudging me after sensing my hesitation.

"Well, I know it may sound silly," I began, "but I'd always imagined I'd be on TV, reporting the news. You know, an anchorwoman, like Jane Pauley on *The Today Show*."

I sounded sheepish, as though I were ashamed of my own dream. It seemed so unreachable to me.

"So, what's stopping *you*?" Frankie didn't blink. Her eyes looked inside of me.

What *was* stopping me? Student loans, not having saved any money, the thought of going back to school, or believing my dreams were either too big or too late for me to grasp all blocked me like a formidable wall. I shrugged and smiled half-heartedly. "I don't know, Frankie. I just haven't figured it out yet."

"Well, *I* believe in you, Juliet. I just know I'm going to see you on the cover of a magazine one day!" She slapped her lap as if the magazine were already there. And just like that, Frankie blew hope into me. I held on to her affirmation like a seed and planted it in the soil of my heart.

I finally held up my hands and said "enough" to Jed's micromanagement and terror tactics. The tension had been building inside me for almost two and a half years now, ever since the very first day I trudged through that murky tour of the department.

One Friday evening in December, the highest volume month for check deposits, I took a longer than usual break to meet family visitors for dinner and stayed out forty-five minutes longer than the one hour I normally took. When I came back from dinner, the other supervisors avoided me like the plague. I knew someone had called Jed, who was off that day, and tattled on me.

The following Monday, Jed marched back into the office and called a team meeting. There we all sat in a dimly-lit, taupe conference room big enough to fit an eight-foot faux wood table and eight chairs. Two rectangular coverings of fluorescent lighting lined the ceiling, spreading sufficient light to only illuminate the table, while leaving shadows pinned to the walls. The room was close to the gated docking station where the couriers delivered batches of checks. My arms prickled with goose bumps as a subtle draft of winter air snuck underneath the door and filled the room with a subtle chill.

"How long of a lunch break did each of you take last Friday?" Jed kicked off the meeting with that question, eyeing each one of us up and down the conference table.

"Thirty minutes," chimed one supervisor on cue.

"Fifteen to twenty minutes," blurted another supervisor, immediately.

"Thirty to forty-five minutes," said a third supervisor, sustaining the quick rhythm of responses.

Then Jed stopped at me and glared. His thin lips pressed together so tightly until it almost appeared he had none.

"About an hour and a half...," I responded, chin up and feeling no shame. I didn't count the extra fifteen minutes of travel time.

"No one takes more than an hour!" he lashed. "I shouldn't have to tell any of you that." He shouted at the team, even though his message was directed at me. Jed ranted for five more minutes before moving on to the next agenda.

The next day, I had a one-on-one with him. He reprimanded me again about taking an extended lunch break, as if I had a long track record of doing it. My body temperature flared as he chastised me like a child. I was always at work, and always rolled up my sleeves to help my team and department achieve its daily deadline. I was a salaried leader on Jed's management team, working at least fifty-five to sixty hours every week. Taking an extended lunch break once in a blue moon didn't equate to a lack of commitment!

"Okay, Jed, but you don't have to yell at me." I shot back. "Going around the table, asking about the length of our lunch breaks...seriously? We're not children!"

Even I was surprised at my courage, how I postured up at that very moment. I had never confronted Jed like that before and wondered if anyone in the department ever had. His eyes bulged with shock, not knowing how to respond. He eventually calmed down and never yelled at me again.

I unloaded to supervisors in other departments about Jed and the oppressive work culture he created. They all just shook their heads while laying a soft hand on my shoulder. One of them suggested I schedule a meeting with the head of Employee Relations, Evelyn Matthews.

And so I did.

To my delight, Evelyn looked like me—a professional, polished woman of color. She was sharply dressed, wearing a pink and mocha tweed double-breasted suit with a fashionable broach pinned to the lapel. Her other accessories, a matching pearl earrings and necklace set, provided the finishing touch of elegance. And while she was statuesque and carried an air of dignity, her smiling eyes revealed an approachable spirit. Right away, I wanted to be her disciple.

"Come on back, Juliet," Evelyn greeted me warmly, as if she had known me for a long time. I met her one day in the mid-morning, an hour before my shift began.

My eyes lit at the bursting rays of sunshine that haloed Evelyn's airy office. It smelled fresh like Pledge lemon-scented polish, unlike the dust that hazed the dungeon. Her space was appointed with sparkling Queen Anne furniture, vintage lamps, and one "hunter and the hound" painting on the eggshell wall behind her traditional desk.

We sat, and I got right down to it. I told Evelyn everything: Jed's bullying, cursing, finger-pointing, and his treating everyone like slaves. She listened patiently with steady eyes, but showed little expression. In fact, her face didn't move at all, and I couldn't tell if she was going through the motions of listening to me, a disgruntled employee, or just flat out didn't care.

Was this the same woman that greeted me?

"Everyone knows Jed's high-strung. But he gets results," Evelyn spoke evenly, matter-of-factly. No one in the company touched Jed because he always made his deadlines in a high-pressure, high-turnover environment. That was his signature.

"Yes, ma'am," I said in a low voice. The room got cold, and fear gnawed at my conscience for ratting on Jed. I didn't want to be a martyr. Shaking, I looked away to hide the tears welling in my eyes.

With a compassionate voice that broke through her tough exterior, Evelyn changed the subject and directed her focus to me. "Tell me more about *you*, Juliet." She spoke with an earthiness so warm and disarming, it relaxed me. The woman that greeted me in the lobby was back.

"Me?" I perked up at Evelyn's nod.

Obediently, I told her a little of my story, about my upbringing in South Carolina and my degree from Spelman College.

"I thought I might go into broadcast journalism. That's what I really thought I'd do, be the next Jane Pauley on *The Today Show* or replace Tom Brokaw on *NBC Nightly News*." My spirit was recharged as I spoke about this dream, and I didn't mind sharing it with Evelyn, who had a therapeutic effect on me.

"You can do whatever you put your mind to." The woman had a velvet touch, an empathy and patience she exuded that made me feel I could talk to her about anything. Like a mother's love, this woman blew hope into my twenty-three-year-old spirit. She leaned back in her chair, smiled, and tilted her head as if she saw something wonderfully magical inside my soul.

And then, Evelyn shared her story with me. She, herself, began her career right out of high school as a teller at the bank, where she worked her way up the ranks to vice president of Employee Relations. She didn't go to college, but that didn't limit her ambition. Smart, savvy, and a loyal soldier, Evelyn possessed a strong gift of discernment and was a great judge of character. People in the company, from the top down, respected and trusted Evelyn, including Jed.

Once, I heard Jed refer to Evelyn as "The Lady" in a reverential sort of way.

"For now," she continued, bringing us both back to the present reality, "you need to go back to your department, to Jed. Learn everything you can from him. Whatever he tells you to do, do it. This is how you grow. *Learn. Everything. You. Can.*"

That voice. She spoke with such distinction. Like autumn, it was rich, soulful, and warm with a pinch of spice. She knew how to get her point across to people.

"And, Juliet, may I give you a final piece of advice?" Evelyn leaned forward, looking straight into my eyes. I nodded, sitting at the edge of my seat, eager to hear what else she had to say. Like an ancient sage, she was full of understanding.

She instructed me to stay away from office gossip. "It's negative. It contaminates you. Whenever you're in the office and the other supervisors complain or spread negativity about Jed, *get up and leave*! Stop talking about Jed to other people. You don't know who's close to whom—you don't know if what you say will get back to him. Do *not* be a part of the conversation."

I pondered Evelyn's words. Many people openly talked about their struggles with Jed. Was that really considered gossip?

"Don't be like everyone else. Be *above* everyone else. Focus on solving problems, not being one."

"What if I don't agree with how things are done?"

"Then leave," she said with a shrug. Evelyn didn't mince words. She spoke to me like a stern-yet-nurturing mother, not like corporate brass. "This isn't your company. Whenever you have a difference in vision, leave and do something else. You won't be happy if you stay, and if you stay with a bad attitude, they'll find a way to get rid of you." Leaning forward, she added one more point to put this issue to bed. "Jed ain't going anywhere. He's in charge because he gets results. Am I clear?"

Yearning for more guidance, my soul just wanted to clasp onto Evelyn and stay in the bright comfort of her well-appointed executive office. But she arose from her chair and tapped her fingers on the desk.

I sighed in quiet dismay. My sunken spirit mustered enough strength to peel away from her and descend back into the dungeon.

Evelyn's truth-telling was a hard pill to swallow. In place of sympathy, she gave me hard knocks. She was a "sistah" looking out for another "sistah," even though she was old enough to be my mother, who was born in and lived through the Civil Rights era. Her generation was of the "be loyal, stable, and 'make your boss look good'" mindset. The only company Evelyn knew was this bank.

But I was much younger and believed in a bigger life. I didn't want to be stuck in a company that sucked the life out of me every day. Even if I weren't on a talk show or other stage, I refused to settle for the consolation prize of working in a basement plantation and staying there for the rest of my life. I was going to be on a stage, be a somebody one day.

Until then, I stuck to Evelyn's advice, kept my attitude in check with Jed, and hung in there. I complied to his leadership, learned everything I could from him, and cultivated useful skills along the way—developing a zero-based budget, reconciling accounts, troubleshooting out-of-service machines, and learning more about how our workflow affected other departments.

Within a few months, Jed promoted me to Officer, gave me a raise, and appointed me to Advisor to new managers going through the same management training program I completed.

And finally, my life began to see some light, especially the moment when a curious fluorescent green flyer with smudged tire tracks caught my attention on an empty parking lot outside a grocery store. The flyer laid beside my car in the bright of day. I noticed the iconic drama masks, one smiling and one frowning, with the words *Community Theatre...audition for a stage play..."*

Instantly, a light bulb went off in my head. It wasn't a TV show, but it was a stage. A silent voice inside me gently said, "Do it," while a cool breeze brushed across my face.

Working a second shift at the bank meant I had almost the entire morning to audition. It was a small play with a small cast and no budget. I bounced on the moon when they told me I landed the leading female role, even though no one else showed up for the audition.

Rehearsals for the play were held inside an old, rundown former movie theatre on the weedy outskirts of I-285 in southwest Atlanta. Faded, partially peeled movie posters loomed sadly on the grimy windows. The theatre sat in a nearly abandoned shopping complex lined with an economy convenience store, a laundromat, a pawnshop, and other small businesses. The parking lot was so cracked and faded the white parking lines were blurred.

Light filled my eyes at the sight of that lonely, broken-down theatre. This was my chance, the opportunity my soul had been craving. A simple start could activate a complex dream.

After a month of rehearsals for the stage play, the cast was ready. I fumbled doing my own makeup and bought thrift clothes suitable for the role, which was a high school teenager battling peer pressure. It was showtime!

Pre-show acknowledgments were made. House lights lowered. Butterflies fluttered fiercely in my stomach. I and the two other hopeful cast members took a deep breath, expecting to see busloads of students and teachers fill up the 150-seat theatre. But once the velvet curtain pulled up, the proverbial drumroll clashed into deflated notes of fading horns.

Eight kids and a teacher had showed up.

Their sparse claps at the end of the show faded inside the hollow theatre. It didn't matter. I still floated after the performance as if Steven Spielberg himself were in the audience.

After that, I hunted with a ravenous appetite for more stage exposure. One day, I was having lunch at a dive in Midtown Atlanta when I saw something in a copy of *Creative Loafing* magazine that made my heart beat achingly fast.

"Ahh!" I gasped while my hands rattled the magazine. There was an advertisement by an acting agency searching for talent of all ages for film roles. Days later, I signed up with the agency for a fee, which paid for my first-ever headshots used to distribute to casting agents.

My heart leaped with each new step—headshots, auditions, rejection, more auditions, and finally, a gig!

With each opportunity landed, I was elated, like a giddy kid going to Disney, even though my roles were nothing more than wallpaper on the film set and I never got paid more than a half a tank of gas.

Start somewhere, I had learned. Then, the momentum will follow. This was how dream activation worked.

Every rising of the sun carried new hope and possibility now. At work one day, I received a serendipitous call from a representative in the bank's internal communications department.

"Hi, Juliet. We're updating our internal dress code catalog. We want to use people from the bank to model for our catalog and your name came up. Are you interested?"

"Sure!" My voice sailed high with so much excitement it was almost shrill.

"Really? That's great." The representative seemed taken aback by my immediate, exuberant response. "It's hard finding people to do this. Many people are actually shy in front of a camera. Evelyn thought you might be a good person for us to ask." She then proceeded to give me the schedule for the photoshoot.

Good ole Evelyn, looking out for me. She may not have ever dropped my name if I hadn't shared my dreams with her.

"Well, I'm so excited. Cameras, lights, stages...I like them. A lot, actually. Happy to do it!"

"Oh, well, in that case, I know we are also working on updating our inclement weather response telephone line. We need a good voice for our recording. You speak very well—so clear and easy on the ear. I can tell just by talking to you. May we use your voice for the recording?"

"Of course!" My heart shot fireworks! The universe kept responding to me. These were small gigs, but I didn't mind. Small opportunities done well eventually lead to other, perhaps bigger, opportunities.

The activity from my outside interests filtered into the bank now, and I floated like a kite. My life finally soared with the belief that I could actually become that dynamic, influential woman of renown in my dreams—until the day those dreams hit a brick wall.

At the bank, an unexpected phone call drained the blood out of me.

"Hi, Juliet. This is Ashley. I'm the assistant vice president of Lockbox. I'm looking forward to working with you. Are you excited?"

I couldn't find my next breath. Was this a prank? Who the heck was this perky, presumptuous voice on the other end of the phone?

"Um, hi, Ashley." I stumbled to find the right words. "Wow... Lockbox? I hadn't heard the news. Jed didn't tell me." My voice deflated quickly. I tightened my grip around the phone, hoping this was a mistake. *I didn't agree to this!*

"Oh, well," Ashley said dismissively, "you're coming! Jed got promoted to assistant vice president and is moving to a different division in the bank. We're consolidating a few departments within our cost centers—and you're coming to Lockbox. When can you start? How about next week?"

I fell back in my chair, stunned. Gratitude for still having a job was eclipsed by this dark hole that grew in the pit of my stomach. The entire exchange was as impersonal as trading baseball cards. The thought of Jed not telling me first was a deeper hurt, as though my feelings or voice didn't matter.

"Let me talk to Jed first," I replied evenly. Lockbox had a reputation, like Jed, for not retaining supervisors. It was another high-pressure production beat. I didn't want to leave one hellhole to go to another. Worse, this department was a first-shift operation which meant I wouldn't have my weekday mornings to audition for any more local stage or film roles.

The pain of separation from losing my baby was unimaginable.

"Okay," Ashley said, rushing me off the phone. "Let me know. See you soon." She swiftly hung up the phone like a completed transaction.

Start Somewhere

The loud click on the other end of the line smacked my eardrum, and immediately a cold sweat broke on my forehead.

I could sense my fate coming to an end at the bank.

CHAPTER 3

Work for a Company That Also Works for You

There was hard determination in my eyes, but I didn't know what to do.

"Going on break, guys," I said. I snatched my London Fog and blazed out of my office, my words like wisps over my shoulder. Alarm mixed with swelling anger painted my face a deep brownish-red after my phone call with Ashley. I heard the muffled sounds of acknowledgment behind me. I'm certain a few employees shot puzzled glances at each other.

"See you soon..." The echo of Ashley's high-pitched voice made me cringe. My body tightened just imagining a high nose and pressed lips on a face that was rigid and hungry for power. I never knew what it meant to be a pawn until now. This was not a change I wanted to make, but I didn't have a choice in the matter. Maybe Ashley didn't, either.

A bigger issue loomed over me. I struggled to find my next breath with the threatening thought of losing something precious. Acting was an outlet and a chance to make steps toward a larger dream. Moving to Ashley's department meant I wouldn't have the flexibility in my schedule to pursue most auditions, many of which were held during the day. How was I to manage that?

I forged my way outside the building. It was late February 1999, and we were still in the thick of winter. I pulled my coat collar tighter around my neck, scanning the cars in the parking lot in search of a sporty, black 1993 Toyota Celica STX, the car I affectionately named "Sassy." Early dusk began to settle with a biting chill that made my squinting eyes water and my breath puff out steam.

Finally, I found it! I marched briskly toward Sassy, but with no immediate plan of where to go.

Light-headed, I gripped the steering wheel to steady myself. My legs weakened as if I were floating, weightless and untethered, like an astronaut who swirls into dark space with a diminishing view of that vibrant marbled planet called home. My heart pounded in fear as darkness swallowed me into a vacuum of uncertainty. Tears welled in my eyes. I was drifting further and further away from the life I had imagined for myself.

The panic I felt was all too familiar. It was like I was a graduating senior at Spelman College all over again, scrambling to find a job. I wanted no more of it! If I had to give up a third of my life each day to earn a living, I wanted to make it count. I determined to plan better and get it right this time.

"Be intentional," I offered, hoping the sound of my own voice would ease me. It didn't. My mind was spinning out of control as I aimlessly drove up and down the streets of Piedmont Avenue.

I imagined what people back home might say or think. Grandma Mattie would not care what I did for a living as long as I had a job that paid the bills and put food on the table. Stability was everything to her. On the other hand, Grandma Ethel might have wanted me to aim higher, pursue a career that garnered more visibility, respect, and was "large-and-in-charge"—achievement and status seemingly mattered to her, even if it meant I married into it.

And then there were the elders and the "mothers" at the church in addition to the neighborhood friends who felt important enough to speak about my life. Their opinions mattered, too, though mostly to my doting grandmothers.

"Humph...humph...humph!" rang their descending notes of disappointment in my mind. "You've only been at that bank for what, three years? They paying you, right? *Chile*...you ungrateful!"

"Julie, now—c'mon...don't disappoint me!" The progressive voice of a pastor-friend, who didn't want me to settle for being an entry-level bank supervisor, reverberated in my mind. "You should be in grad school somewhere, or law school. You're capable of more...much more!"

But the comments that seared my confidence the most were the real, not imagined, subtle slaps that came whenever I was compared to my sister. It wasn't uncommon—and said far too often—for well-meaning elders and distant family to approach us with this annoying question: "Which one of you is the doctor?"

Annette finished medical school and became the family's pride, including mine. The "MD" beside her name lifted her high in the eyes of others and made her a star. The burn I felt was never out of envy or jealousy—I was Annette's biggest cheerleader and loved her more than anybody did. She was my big sister. I always believed I was just as smart, if not smarter than she. I mean, after all, I graduated valedictorian in my class—Annette graduated salutatorian in hers. No, it was the feeling of being dismissed, as if I were a low achiever. Directly or indirectly, being compared to my sister's achievements made me feel small, unimportant, and sometimes, invisible.

I snapped myself back to reality. Instinctively, my car made a left turn at a traffic light and into my favorite restaurant, located a few blocks from my job. I parked my car neatly within the white crisp parking lines that glowed even now as the sun was falling. This restaurant always kept a clean, tight lot with manicured shrubs, as if it had just opened up on its first day for business. It was the only chain I trusted because the restrooms were clean. I ate there almost every day.

With staccato steps, I dashed from my car to find warmth inside. Only a few people were in the dining room, where tables and chairs stood perfectly aligned, and absolutely no debris of paper or crumbs could be spotted on the glistening tile floor. The subtle aroma of fresh baked bread disarmed me like a hug at Grandma's house, and I knew in that moment I was safe.

My shoulders relaxed when a young smiling face locked eyes with mine and approached me to take my order.

"What can I get for you today?" she asked, looking at me with energetic confidence. Her name, Priya, was printed in white letters on her red rectangular badge and pinned to her white collared shirt. A yellow perky bow completed her look.

I didn't know why I stared at the menu. There wasn't much variety in it, and I always got the same thing—a club sandwich combo with my favorite drink in the world, sweet tea, the wine of the South.

"Umm," I hesitated, like I always do, as if I dared to order something different. "Let me get the club combo—with a sweet tea."

"Okay!" Priya said, as she repeated my order and the amount with a burst of enthusiasm. I'd never heard anyone else in a casual restaurant be so excited to take my order before. Behind the counter with Priya were two other young workers who moved with pep. I caught the smiles they sporadically flashed at each other.

I handed Priya my money while one of the other restaurant workers at the bagging station presented my tray of food and drink to me before I could put my wallet back inside my purse.

"Here you go...enjoy!" Priya said, beaming. "Let me know if I can get anything else for you!"

"Thanks." I managed a polite nod at her as she continued to smile winningly as if I were her favorite customer.

I found an empty table beside a corner window and put my tray down. I opened the sandwich and yanked my hand away from the spraying steam. I squeezed a couple of strips of mayonnaise onto my buttered bread, then reassembled my sandwich, blew on it, and took a small bite, followed by a quick wash of cold sweet tea. Immediately, I exhaled and closed my eyes, comforted by the warm saltiness, crunchiness, and the ascension to a sugar high. I almost made it to heaven until my mind flashed back to that call from Ashley.

My shoulders tightened again. I rested my sandwich on the tray and peered outside the window in a blank daze. It was now total darkness save the speckled lights from moving cars and shopping center marquees.

I never realized how being overlooked and ignored could produce such a deep hurt. I was to be shipped off to a foreign environment with no previous announcement, advance notice, or courtesy of a one-on-one meeting with Jed, my current manager, for him to tell me, "Hey, Juliet, I've got a new opportunity for you. Let's talk about it...."

Stunned and clueless, my brows furrowed, searching for answers. This bank, what I'm doing...it's *not* me, and it's not *for* me, I thought. Outside, more cars arrived in the parking lot. My eyes blurred into red taillights as my mind began to wander once more.

There I was, standing on a hardwood stage soaked in the spotlight, smiling and speaking to an audience I couldn't see. Inside the blackness purred soft ruffles of laughter, followed by captivated silence, then robust applause. In a white flash, my dreams traveled to another scene where I sat in front of a camera on a set with teleprompters. My smile beamed rays that stretched through the lens. Then, my mind skirted to other visions, where I saw myself in magazines and at premieres—a red carpet darling in a fairy-tale gown.

"Do you like your sandwich?"

"What?" I was so deep in thought I didn't notice her standing there. Her voice alone was a pleasant pull back into reality, though I preferred to stay camped in my dreams. Priya glanced down at my food then raised her thick, threaded eyebrows with polite curiosity.

"The sandwich? Is there anything else I can get for you?"

"Oh!" I shook my head and reached for it. "Yes, it's great." I hoped my smile saved me from coming across as dismissive.

Priya waltzed away to chat with other customers before returning to her register to take more orders. She was a walking hearth, I noticed, radiating joy throughout the restaurant. I'd never seen this before in other fast food restaurants, where encounters with employees were usually impersonal and transactional, like my telephone experience with Ashley.

Coldness went through me, again, at the thought.

I yearned to be the woman in my dreams, but I just didn't know how to find her. What career did she have? What office did she occupy? How did she make money? I was off course and lost like an abandoned ship adrift on a dark sea.

Being on a stage was where the sun kissed me. I remembered feeling this way when I practiced public speaking in high school. It was where I felt the most alive—and one of the ways I stood out among my peers. I knew I possessed a natural ability to use my voice to captivate and bring meaning to other people's lives, and it felt good. I just didn't know how to translate it into a career.

At first, I thought it was broadcast journalism. Being forced to watch the news every night as a teenager inspired me to believe I could become a broadcaster like Tom Brokaw or Jane Pauley. I figured broadcast journalism was a specialized discipline that had to be studied in college, but I hadn't taken advantage of opportunities while in school to put myself in that environment. And so, I gave up on that dream and settled for a steady paying job at the bank.

Whereas acting, well, not all actors studied acting. Many fell into it or "crossed over" from a different career. Acting felt tangible, perhaps more possible than a career in broadcast journalism. And it was still a stage.

"Well, if you really want to act, you have to go where the actors are," Evelyn said once. I recalled her telling me that as I went on small auditions. Always frank, she knew I was unhappy at the bank.

But I trembled at the thought that California would eat me alive. It was too expensive to live there and too far away from home and anything familiar. Growing up in the Bible Belt, I'd heard stories of broke, starving actresses who'd sold their souls to the devil to get a part in a movie. *Not me!*

If only Hollywood were in Atlanta....

I shrank in the chair at my own lack of courage, thinking my dream might actually be more of a pipe dream. Pressure mounted within me to make the world see me as valid and bona fide.

There was no other choice but to find another place of employment. I refused to get "locked" into banking or become a wandering supervisor, laterally moving from one department to the next.

It was time to find work that also worked for me.

"But where?" I muttered under my breath. And more importantly, what?

My sigh stretched as far as a country mile. I expected to hear an audible voice whisper the answer in my ear. But instead, my ears filled with a rise of indistinct chatter from customers who poured into the restaurant and occupied the tables around me.

Since Hollywood was out of the question, I racked my brain for movie-related jobs in Atlanta that would give me status and more income than what I was making at the bank. But all I came up with was Blockbuster Video. Something about that company didn't fit.

"I don't want to just exist, I want to *live*." I mouthed those words emphatically in my reflective state. *Be intentional*, I thought again, pressing my lips. I was determined not to compromise. Living life on my own terms meant more to me than any amount of money and any title!

I took a sip of my sweet tea and relished the thought of being in control of my life. No more would I send out a bunch of resumes like I did in college, in desperation, hoping that someone would take me. I was going to choose where I wanted to go this time.

No more oppressive cultures. The company's values, or principles, would have to be consistent with mine.

And never again did I want to work around people with faces so long they swept the floor. I wanted to follow leaders who inspired me, not intimidated me like Jed. I wanted to grow and develop as a leader with opportunities for upward mobility. It was a bonus if the company provided tuition reimbursement. At some point I knew I would go back to school to get a graduate degree, though not now.

Principles, people, and...

The light bulb turned on once more. My lips curved upward, and my heart started beating again. I was on to something. Of course! I needed to believe in what the company produced. And banking never excited me. I never cared about another person's money.

Principles, people, and product. Those were my terms. I had a template now to base which companies I would consider applying to.

But I was stuck. I still didn't really know, outside of a stage or movies, what excited me or what brands I cared about the most. I clearly didn't know myself too well at twenty-four.

Thinking hard, I picked up my sandwich and took another bite, and then my eyes grew.

It hit me!

"Ahh!" I said to myself in sheer wonder, looking at the sandwich in my hand like a winning lottery ticket. "I can get excited about this!" It dawned on me that I might actually be holding the answer to my question. Why not pursue a career with *this* growing restaurant company, a place I come to almost every day?

And like a wave of a wand, my dull, black-and-white view brushed into full, bright Technicolor. I sat up straight in my chair, wide-eyed, as a tidal wave of peace and invigorated energy gushed over me.

My gaze immediately shot over to Priya, a spring of happiness, who seemed to move like a gazelle among her fellow employees behind the counter. Her smile never left her, and I marveled at my own recollection of never having a bad experience with any employee at this restaurant. In fact, the whole team behind the counter leaned into each other, like they really enjoyed working here. I had never witnessed this level of enthusiasm at any other food establishment.

I looked at the menu board, where there was a primary focus on sandwiches, something this business got right. Seemingly, they chose to specialize in one thing and be great at it.

Everything about the restaurant boasted excellence from my view in the dining room. It helped me see that this was a company worth pursuing. If it was this great at the franchise level, I couldn't help but imagine what the corporate office might be like, where the decisions were made.

My body was electric now. Adrenaline pumped into it as my sights shifted toward this company with much interest and possibility.

I rushed out of the restaurant excited to begin my process of courting my potential new employer.

I now had a plan.

Every day was an eternity. Physically, I arrived at the bank every morning by seven-thirty to kick off the morning shift at Lockbox. Mentally, I was gone.

Lockbox was a service the bank provided to other companies, whereby the bank received, processed, and deposited a company's receivables. My office was at a different location, close to the airport on Virginia Avenue, in a mid-rise brick building with lots of windows that actually felt more corporate than the dungeon I had known for the past three years. Light filled the department, a massive flat square floor, and there was a slight sense of calm. There were no bustling loud machines nor paper dust hanging in the air. I actually started wearing suits again.

Ashley was an assistant vice president with the bank. She didn't bark or hover over me like Jed. In fact, I barely saw her. She was always in someone else's meeting. Every other Wednesday, she touted a standing manicure appointment from one to two o'clock.

She looked like she was in her late thirties or early forties, as evidenced by the crow's feet gently etched in the corners of her pale green eyes. Her high-pitched shrill rarely pierced the air, and none of the processors seemed to be affected by her presence. I wondered if they even knew who she was. Ashley didn't refer to any of the processors by name, but she definitely knew the names of the supervisors who reported to her—at least one of them.

"This is Ray," Ashley said, introducing me to her lead supervisor, a *brutha*. "Ray will get you up to speed here. We're glad to have you!" And off Ashley went.

Ray chuckled with a slight shake of his head. He caught how my eyes narrowed at Ashley's back. We started walking through the aisles of the floor.

"How long have you worked in Lockbox?"

"Ten years."

My mouth dropped to the floor.

"Ten years as a supervisor. I started out as a processor." Ray's head lifted as he said that.

I simply nodded as we kept walking. He introduced me to all the processors, whom he knew by name. He exchanged smiles with every single one of them, touching a few of them on the shoulder, and I knew then that Lockbox wasn't Ashley's department. It was Ray's.

I'm not sure why I thought Lockbox was another hellhole. It had a reputation for being one, when in fact, the environment was an upgrade from Jed's department.

Production environments inside this bank, I eventually realized, carried a stigma. They projected a picture of an advanced assembly line, monotonous work, long hours (you don't go home until the last check is processed), and a labor force of processors who were mostly Black or people of color. Lockbox was only a hellhole to uppity people like Ashley, who preferred not to get close to the very people that made her look good.

For five months, each day was a waiting game. I mustered as much strength as I could to maintain a positive attitude, but I simply did not want to be there. Showing up to work with a smile was a lie. Deep down, I was anything but happy. I didn't even try to invest time with any of the processors to learn their stories. My heart was not in it.

I checked my home voice messages often to see if there was good news from the restaurant company to tell me, "We'd like you to join our team...."

But over the course of five months, the messages they left, which came every two to three weeks, were to schedule yet another interview. I had already met with thirteen people. The company told me on day one that its selection process took a while.

"Be patient," was a common response from its representatives. "It takes a while to become a part of our company. We take our time with people...like a courtship."

Funny choice of words, I thought, as I approached my application pursuit the same way. "If we like you and you like us, it's like going to the altar," they told me.

I was ready to wear happiness on my face without the help of a mask, like Priya, whom I never saw again because I worked at a different office building on a different side of town. My heart warmed at the thought of her.

I had already decided that night in the restaurant that I was going to take a monogamous approach to my job search. No more spreading my resumes around hoping to get lucky. I determined to take my time, do my research, and make sure the company I wanted to work for would also work for me according to my terms—principles, people, and product.

I patiently waited, leaning on inspirational gospel music to revive my spirit. It was difficult going through the motions. I often took naps in Sassy in the parking lot during my lunch break to quiet my mind. Each day when I got home, I was so mentally exhausted from playing the happy, "be grateful" game that I immediately went to bed and slept until it was time to go back the next day. Whether this restaurant company offered me a career or not, my soul confirmed my days at the bank were winding down. I just couldn't visualize myself there much longer.

And then one day, about four weeks later, the company called me to schedule a final interview with a vice president of the company. I couldn't sit still! I knew it was a positive sign and that I was close to an offer!

The interview was short, more like an introduction and conversation.

"I want to talk you out of a job," said the elder, balding vice president sitting across from me, smiling.

I shook my head, matching my smile to his. "I want to be here, Sir. I've waited months to sit in this seat. It took too long to get here. There's no way I'm backing out!" I was as ecstatic as Tom Cruise's character at the time of his mega job offer in *The Firm*.

The elder executive laughed at my lighthearted humor, although I was dead serious.

The following week, I received a serendipitous phone call at my office from one of the group leaders at the company who interviewed me. His name was Josh.

"Well, Juliet, are you ready to come and join us?" Josh's words were warm and fatherly. I knew right away I would love working with him. "When can you start?"

"Yes, Josh, absolutely!" I wasn't used to someone asking me about a start date. I was accustomed to such information being dictated to me. "Um...I just need to give the bank a two-week notice, and then I can start right away!" The day I waited for had finally come—six months and fourteen interviews from the moment I faxed my resume and cover letter to the company.

"You sure? You mean you don't want a few weeks to take a break before you come?" I melted at the sound of Josh's voice, so warm and caring.

"Well," I hesitated. "Maybe just a week off after I turn in my notice. That'll do." I was champing at the bit. "So, three weeks. Is that okay?"

"Okay, then. Sure! I'm really looking forward to you joining us!"

We both hung up the phone, and immediately I raced to my office computer and printed my two-week notice. Beaming, I waltzed into Ashley's office and placed my two-week notice into her perfectly manicured hands. Her eyes widened. With pursed lips, she cleared her throat.

"Wow...well, I guess this means good luck to you." She didn't seem happy for me. To her, I was probably just another supervisor to come and go. In fact, she escorted me out of the building fifteen minutes later. "Bank policy," she said. Of course, I knew better. It was only bank policy to escort the resigned employee immediately if going to work for another bank.

There was no fond farewell, no message to staff, and no appreciation expressed for my service to the bank. I didn't even have a chance to tell anyone goodbye. I was just another transaction, like I was from the very beginning, when Ashley called to tell me I'd be working in Lockbox.

Ray called me the next day.

"What happened?"

"I got another job!" I squealed the good news to him. "I gave Ashley my two-week notice. She decided I didn't have to work it. Escorted me out of the building."

"She didn't have to do that." I could hear him shaking his head.

"I get paid regardless."

"Yeah, you mean you get a vacation!" His tone lightened with laughter. "Well, congratulations, Juliet. I'm going to miss you."

The next day and for several days thereafter, I woke up in a surreal state not knowing what to do with my time now that my employment at the bank had ended. I had a total of three weeks of nothingness since Ashley had relieved me from working out my notice. I thought I would be jumping up and down on the bed, but instead, I laid curled, clutching my pillow with my face soaked in tears. I was paralyzed in a dark hole.

The closing of the bank chapter was like a death. I should have been celebrating freedom, but instead, I only felt this gaping hollowness in my heart. Breaking away from familiarity—good or bad—left me with much anxiety. Separation made my soul ache with much sorrow. It was like the tears flowing after graduating from high school or college; you're sad to leave the people who had become fixtures in your life—sometimes, even the mean and toxic ones.

"You won! Remember?" I pepped myself in the bathroom mirror one day. "You did it. Don't look back." My words didn't heal the scars right away, though. I cried for about three days.

On my first day of work with my new employer, my mobile phone rang just as I was pulling into the parking lot. I was shocked to hear a familiar voice on the other end when I answered. It was my talent agent.

"Juliet, where have you been? We need to update your headshots. And there is an audition at the Cartoon Network that I want you to go to."

An audition? I hadn't had any auditions or roles in the last six months, ever since I moved to the Lockbox Department at the bank. Working a regular nine-to-five shift didn't give me that flexibility. As I sat in the parking lot on the first day of starting my new job, I froze at the thought of doing one more audition. What if...?

There, I was faced with a choice. I turned my car off and glanced through the sprawling trees that draped the mid-rise company building. Was this a sign or a test?

Do I choose my dream, or a job with guaranteed growth and golden benefits?

My new job just seemed too good to let go or even half-step with it. After all, it checked all my boxes, and I endured fourteen interviews over six months to get it. It was as if the glassy building stared back at me, waiting for me to respond.

I heard birds chirping and watched as gleeful people, dressed in professional business attire, skipped inside the building.

"Juliet? Still there?" asked my agent.

Maybe my dreams were waiting for me inside that building, I pondered. Maybe God had a stage in that company that could be mine one day. I owed it to myself to give it my all and find out. I had waited too long for this moment and was determined to make it count.

"Nah, no thanks," I told my agent. "I just started a new job. I'm here now. I'm going to focus on where I am."

"Humph. Well, then...okay. Good luck," she said. Her tone was just as final as mine.

I never heard from her again.

I got out of Sassy and walked down the wooded path to join the happy faces filing into the building, hoping to one day discover myself.

CHAPTER 4

Become Your Own Champion

"We should all go to the Wild at Heart Men's Conference together!"

Jackson, once a pastor and former Boy Scouts troop leader, stood at attention at the head of the table, holding up a handful of glossy brochures about the conference. He scanned the other faces, nodding in either consideration or in agreement with the idea.

Except his eyes never met mine.

Out of the six of us, I was the only woman and person of color in the room.

A wisp of coldness blew through me.

"This could be our team bonding trip for next year!" Jackson continued. "We'll be up in the Colorado mountains—go hiking and camping—and there'll be great leadership development. We'll have fun and come back better as husbands and fathers... and leaders."

"Yeah, Jackson, that's a great idea!" declared Duke, another teammate. A couple of men dropped their mouths and raised their eyebrows at Duke, who typically projected an air that great ideas could only come from him. But everyone knew Duke loved anything involving the outdoors, rifles, and water. He often bragged about his hunting trips.

The idea thrilled me, too. I had never been to Colorado before, nor many places, for that matter. My heart filled with excitement at the possibility of experiencing the majestic beauty I only knew from magazines.

But Jackson said it was a *men's* retreat.

My head slowly fell as I attempted to conceal my furrowed brows. I sat motionless in my chair while a different kind of awkwardness swelled inside me.

It was the sort of uneasiness anyone might feel if expected to intelligently respond to a question without fully having all the information—and not knowing where the other person was coming from. All I knew to do was smile. Just smile. Whenever in doubt, that was my first step in getting through awkward situations while disarming the adversary.

The only problem was, at the moment, my usual winning smile was nowhere to be found.

It was my first fall planning retreat with my team. I was somewhere in North Georgia on the rustic grounds of a tucked-away lodge and conference center. I was excited to experience a real retreat instead of being locked inside a bland meeting room all day. A glorious canvas of burnt orange and honey-colored trees serenaded the facilities—a far cry from the noisy, dusty basement I knew at the bank.

After leaving the bank a little over a year ago, I had grasped the promise of a dream career with a growing company that took me six months and fourteen interviews to land. I pranced in this new world of employment, where teams traveled to adventurous places and called it work.

The agenda item up for discussion now was what activities we were going to do together to build and bond our team for the upcoming 2001 calendar year.

Here I was, excited that I had "arrived"—until this moment. The room's brightness shaded into a soft gray, and I suddenly grew numb. The idea of my attending a men's conference, as a woman, somehow didn't sit too well with me. No energy was directed my way, however, not even a slight acknowledgment of my presence.

As the newest consultant on the team, I wanted so badly to fit in, be accepted, and just be "one of the boys." But how could I, a twenty-something-year-old Black woman, fit in with a homogenous display of older White men whose average age was forty?

I fidgeted in my seat, wrestling with this idea. But I wanted them to like me. I swallowed a deep breath, cleared my throat, and decided to go along.

"I guess it could be good...um...for me, too—to attend a men's conference." My lone, tremulous voice found its way into the conversation. "It might help me to understand men better, to learn how men communicate...you know...how you guys think...."

Suddenly, there was silence.

It was the first time I'd spoken up. I glanced around the table with a nervous smile. Rapid heartbeats pounded through my chest. All I got back in return were averted glances, though I noticed a few exchanged uneasy looks with each other. Duke rolled his eyes.

But Jackson was as unmoved as his stiff, gelled silvery hair. The lines etched in his forehead didn't bend when he finally looked at me.

"Oh...you can't go," he said, without blinking an eye. He stood erect at the head of the conference table as if he were commander in chief, even though in reality we were all teammates. "It's a men's conference...for men only. Women aren't allowed."

My lips pursed at his response while my eyes grew in horrific disbelief. I shifted my gaze toward the windows, where the trees seemingly hunched together in sorrow for me. Leaves dropped incessantly like tears. I gulped so loudly that it could be heard a mile away.

"I'm sorry, but you can't go," he repeated with cool, unwavering poise, as if I were out of order for thinking I could.

"So, then, a *team* outing...without Juliet?" I shot back.

I'm not sure where I got the courage to challenge Jackson. But I sat firmly in my chair, unapologetically, in a stare-down contest with him.

A tense silence permeated the room. No one moved. A couple of eyes lowered while others whispered, *"Oh, damn!"*

Had I just spiraled into *The Twilight Zone*? It was as if my entire world were brought into a black-and-white throwback of the 1950s, when a "Whites only" sign could have been easily posted on the conference room door.

"Let's take a fifteen-minute break!" interjected T.J., another one of my teammates. He was the team's peacekeeper and quiet sage.

"Yep!" Most of the consultants eagerly complied. Immediately, they scrambled out of their chairs and scattered in different directions, while Jackson smacked the glossy brochures on the table.

I, too, hopped out of my seat and dashed to the ladies' lounge. My heart raced with either panic or anger—I was not sure which. Shaking, I hid myself inside the farthest empty bathroom stall and locked it. I struggled to find my next breath.

A lump formed in my throat as I pressed my head against the stall door. With muffled sobs, I squeezed my eyes shut and wrapped my arms tightly around my chest. Wet lines began to streak down my soft brown face. This was my first bathroom moment.

Training was over. There was no more euphoria about being a new hire with this company. The smiles and warm hellos I experienced in my interviews now seemed as artificial as the mannequins in a store window. Behind closed doors breathed something extremely peculiar, unlike anything I had ever experienced in my young career—or life.

I didn't see this one coming. Or, did I?

A different type of Goliath was coming into focus, one that was either hidden or dormant during the multiple interviews I'd nailed to get this job. There was no yelling, pointing fingers, cussing, or tyrannical tantrums like the ones that colored my experience at the bank.

No, this one was civil, yet it penetrated a deep hurt. It was like I was up against an invisible wall. Or maybe *I* was the invisible one. Even though I was there, sitting at the table, I was as inconspicuous to them as a corner figurine or a portrait on a wall.

I broke out into a cold sweat and continued to tremble in the bathroom stall.

Did I do something wrong already? I racked my brain wondering why Jackson and the others would assume it was fine to leave me out of the team bonding trip.

Or was I simply foolish to pursue employment with this company? I thought I had done my homework. All the right boxes were checked—principles, people, and product. Was this company going to work for me after all?

I reflected on the stats I knew. Here we were, in Y2K, and there were no women or people of color on the executive committee. Out of approximately 450 employees in the office, only one Black man occupied a vice president role in the company. There was one Black woman who was an accounting group leader, and then three to four people of color on a manager-grade level, including me. I might have recalled one or two Latino and Asian corporate employees along the way.

That should have been a hint. There were other hints, too, of this new Goliath. I caught glimpses of it during my training. I was the only person of color in my training class of twenty-two people or so. It wasn't long before the curious opposition targeted me.

"How are *you*, a Black woman, going to work with us White men?" a guy in my training class asked me, scratching his bushy head. He wasn't mean or malicious—actually, he was a gregarious personality who strutted around in class like a self-proclaimed statesman—but his question still pierced my heart like an arrow. I was shocked into silence, not knowing what to say, while a few of my classmates within earshot lowered their heads.

On another occasion, a lean elderly man approached me in the building atrium as I was headed toward the dining hall for lunch. I wasn't sure which department he worked in, but I saw him often around the building. His eyes always seemed to follow me. I greeted him nervously as he stopped in front of me, blocking my path to the lunch line with a questioning look.

"You know, Juliet, I look at you...and I just wonder..." He tilted his head and narrowed his eyes before continuing in his sharp country twang. "I think 'bout Carla—she can challenge men. Then there's Vicki...she'll do alright, I reckon. But *you*, I just see...a great big smile."

I wasn't smiling at the moment.

"I'm wondering...can *you* really challenge and help men lead their work? Hmm?"

His words drained the blood out of me. My mouth slightly dropped. Both Carla and Vicki were Black. In fact, the three of us were the *only* female consultants in our department, though we each served on different teams. And while I wasn't anything like them, I was being compared to them, and, perhaps, expected to be their clone.

A burn raked through me. I didn't know what I resented more—his shallow assumptions of me or the fact that he was emboldened to share them. This man and I worked in different departments; he hadn't spent any time to get to know me. I wondered how he might have felt if a random person, who knew very little about him, stopped *him* in his tracks to say, "Hey, dude...I don't think you have the balls to do your job!"

Of course, I could never say that. I was the new kid on the block in a very visible and influential role that was mostly occupied by White men. My young body froze as I looked up into the squinted eyes of this graying man. I swallowed hard before flashing him a wry smile.

"Well," I said softly, "first of all, I'm not Carla—nor Vicki. And secondly, I interviewed with a lot of people to get here. My leader believes in me—he thinks I can do this job. And *his* boss, the senior vice president, supports me, too. So, if *they* think I can do this job, then *I* think I'll be just fine!"

A slight brush of red painted his leathered face. He darted his eyes across me, and after a slight scoff, he left.

I did my best to steady myself as I proceeded to lunch. I grabbed my tray and ate in the still sanctity of my office, alone, in tears, where I quietly toyed with my food.

The distant, squishing sound of toilets accompanied by male chatter on the other side of the bathroom wall interrupted my bleak reverie. I grabbed some toilet paper to wipe my face and blow my nose. I glanced quickly at my watch. Ten more minutes remained in the break.

I remained glued in the stall. I thought about calling Vicki, who was a few years older than me and the only woman and person of color on her team, too. She was a straight shooter, yet still possessed a velvet touch with people. We often exchanged stories of work-life in my office, and at this moment, I desperately needed her encouragement.

As if my anxiety weren't high enough, she didn't answer on my first attempt. What was I thinking? She was probably in a planning meeting like me. But I didn't care. I hit the redial button continuously like a mad stalker and refused to leave a message. When she finally picked up, I gave her the play-by-play of the meeting and my confrontation with Jackson.

Vicki didn't say much. She just listened. Maybe my story triggered flashbacks to her own uncomfortable workplace experiences, maybe she was just in shock, or maybe she was just annoyed because I had called a trillion times back-to-back.

There was a brief silence at first. Then, a sigh.

"Hmm...I'm sorry that happened," Vicki said in a soft, gentle tone that reflected her dismay. "It's not right, but I know exactly how you feel. What are you going to do?"

Hell, I don't know. That's why I'm calling you! But what else could she really say?

I was in the big leagues. In this game, there was no running to others for help or a handout—at least not for me. It was clear I had to work out this situation for myself. I had to carry my own water.

"I don't know," I sighed, sinking back against the tiled wall. I was still relieved just to hear a friendly, soothing voice on the other line. "I guess I just needed to talk to somebody."

Sometimes, it just sucks being the "only one." The journey is so lonely.

"Hang in there," Vicki said.

I mustered enough strength from that phone call to keep my sanity. I slowly unlocked the bathroom stall door and stood in front of the bathroom mirror, took a deep breath, and looked into my own molten-brown eyes.

Was I strong enough to go back in there? "Yes."

What was I supposed to do to get their respect? "It's not about them. It's about me, about how *I* show up! Be yourself and stand your ground."

Was God with me? "Always. He promised to never leave me nor forsake me."

Sometimes, you just have to talk to yourself.

Because the truth was, I *needed* this job. I couldn't just "jump." I had bills and student loans to pay. Not every twenty-six-year-old got this kind of opportunity, the opportunity to be gainfully employed by a respected brand and given responsibilities to influence $60 million dollars of business. One person, or a team of people, was *not* going to make me give that up...not today.

I took a deep breath and tightened my ponytail. With my head up, I firmly footed myself back into the conference room, ready to face Goliath.

As soon as everyone else sat at the table, T.J. evenly said, "I don't think we should go to the men's conference as a team bonding trip. Let's find something we can *all* do together."

No one challenged T.J. It was clear they had already discussed and decided this among themselves while I was alone in the bathroom stall. Jackson pursed his lips and said nothing.

I exhaled. My chin lifted slightly.

And that was the end of it...on *that* day.

I liked Josh. No, I *loved* him.

He was my group leader, respected by the company for his gentle wisdom and ability to build people. I was truly grateful to have him as my boss. His encouraging words wrapped around me like a warm blanket; his commitment to my growth was as bottomless as his gray-green eyes.

I didn't have a crush on Josh—he was more like a father figure. Like a doe-eyed teenager, I adored him as a daughter does her brave father, and wanted to believe he embraced me as one of his own. He often joked with me about how he committed the cardinal sin in our interview.

"You remind me of one of my girls," he said. I didn't remember what I had said that struck a fond chord with him. Perhaps it was my humor, spunk, or vivacious spirit. Or, maybe in my youthful inexperience, he spotted a dogged determination, a fire in my belly, a type of grit or fearlessness in my eyes. Either way, he *saw* me and made me feel safe. And I loved him for it.

"I know you don't have a lot of experience, Juliet." Josh came into my office one day and, per his custom, leaned his long limbs against my desk rather than sit in my chair. He often popped in to either give feedback or to just simply check in. His visits were like comfort food, his words smooth as water. "You're green, but I see in you a lot of raw talent. Talent that can be developed over time. Just keep doing what you're doing and hang in there. You're special."

Josh was a needed salve when days in the office were a series of paper cuts. He often restored my hope that I *did* belong on his team. After all, he chose me when he could have selected anybody else. That meant something to me.

I determined to not let Josh down and labored to gel with the team despite my own discomforts. I'm sure Josh strongly encouraged the men to reach out to me, too. Building teams was his trademark.

I accepted every invitation to attend a teammate's dinner, child's basketball game, family wedding, and any other event that was extended, probably out of obligation. It didn't matter. I showed up because I wanted to feel like I belonged, to become more familiar and likeable to the men who surrounded my work daily.

But it was exhausting as hell. I often held my breath attending their family events, especially as a single woman. I was usually the only Black person at their functions. I looked around the room and often wondered if they knew *anybody*, other than me, that didn't look like them.

Still, I never pulled the race card with Josh. I didn't "tattle-tale" to him about my feelings about the team. I just wore my smile and kept up a picture that all was well, even though I often sat on tacks in meetings anticipating the next insensitive remark I might hear regarding people—and their classifications of them.

Duke, especially, wielded an air of superiority. He often looked down on others, it seemed, even though he stood inches below everyone else in the room. "I will *not* be treated like a second-class citizen!" he loudly exclaimed whenever other leaders pulled rank over him.

I couldn't help but wonder if he saw me that way, as a second-class citizen. He never really asked for my thoughts and perspectives on matters in team meetings. He sometimes rolled his eyes whenever I spoke up and boiled if I dared to challenge him on an issue.

Duke wasn't a bad person, though. He just lived and operated inside his bubble, a product of the environment he knew. He and another teammate came to my rescue once when Sassy blew a tire on the drive to work. I was along the side of the highway, and I didn't know how to change a tire. Duke got out of his car with a big smile holding a carnation of flowers, while the other teammate changed my tire. I knew then that underneath Duke's hardened pride existed a treasure of goodness.

"That's a quality I appreciate about you," Josh often told me. "You don't get defensive."

Yeah, I'm sure Josh could only imagine how I was feeling at times, how it was a wonder that I could keep smiling. He was an Anglo baby boomer who lived through the Jim Crow era. Now, in the twenty-first century, he finally desegregated *his* team by onboarding me.

If only he could walk in my shoes. If only he could taste desolation.

I bottled all of my frustrations, like those moments when emails to the team began with "Gentlemen." Those moments when we would be offsite at a company function, and all of them spontaneously huddled together a few feet away from me appearing to talk about something important. Or the times in meetings when my comments were interrupted, talked over, or left unacknowledged altogether. If only Josh knew.

"Well, Josh, you know..." I exhaled into a smile. "I'm just grateful to be here. And, well—your feedback and support mean a lot." I paused to swallow the lump that was forming in my throat. "I just want to make you proud."

Josh stood on his feet, and I got up from my chair. He gave me a warm hug.

"You *do* make me proud!" he chuckled. "You're so coachable." Before leaving my office, he turned around and said, "For the next year, just keep learning and asking questions. That's how you'll grow, and for now, that's all I expect."

And learn, I did.

I needed to tighten up on my follow-up—Josh had given me some feedback on that. He let me listen to a voicemail once where a senior officer in the company briefly noted I didn't follow up on something.

"Don't let that become an issue," Josh said. "If someone calls you out on something—especially more than twice—just make sure you correct it right away so that it doesn't become an issue. So, go to that person right now and give her what she asked for. And say to her, 'I'm following up...here you go.' Just do that. That's what I did when someone said that about me—that I didn't follow up on stuff. That was early in my career. I made sure that never became an issue again."

That was Josh. He never bashed. He only coached.

Team meetings were a different matter. It was more than just building and protecting the brand, it was a classroom on distinctions and the mindset of the privileged. Every month, during the "catch-up" time in team meetings, I listened to their stories of golf outings, hunting trips, camping adventures, weekend trips to lake houses, or how their kids were doing in expensive private schools. Many of their wives didn't work outside the home.

I was perplexed. How much money did you have to make to live like that? Certainly not on the $50,000 they paid me as a junior consultant. This was a world I only saw in movies and never thought existed in real life. No one at the bank ever told those stories, not even Jed. I just sat there most of the time in feigned amusement of the people who lived at the top of the food chain. It was no wonder they didn't see me—I didn't exist up there.

Homes were a big deal, too. It reflected the size and weight of their "kingdoms." I would have never thought that coworkers cared so deeply about where each other lived—it was like a competition. But I wasn't at the bank anymore. I was in a peculiar land with people who lived life together outside the company walls.

I discovered there were approved places to live...and unapproved places. People weren't perceived as smart, clean, or pretty if they lived in the "unapproved" places. I cringed whenever I heard their labels of certain parts of Atlanta.

"Eww, that place is *rough*!" they would say. Or, "It's very *dark* over there."

"Rough" areas were defined as the absence of "good" public schools. And "good" often meant very little diversity.

"You know...some people believe where you live determines *how* you live," the wife of one of my teammates casually once told me.

It was no wonder they were unimpressed when I bought my first house in the "hood."

But I didn't think it was a hood. In fact, I thought I had accomplished something extraordinary. I bought a single-family house in a one-street neighborhood shortly after I completed my training with the company. In my mid-twenties, I had saved enough money to close on my first starter home in a cul-de-sac with no help from family or a sugar daddy. With a few updates, I believed I could make it into a great house for me. There was no sprawling golf course in my backyard nor any Olympic-size swimming pool—just a bunch of shaggy trees. I did it on my own with money I had saved, and I was proud. We all have to start somewhere.

But it was in an area that made people wrinkle their narrow haughty noses. It was east of Atlanta, outside the I-285 perimeter, where development lagged compared to other parts of the metropolitan city. Outside my subdivision on the main street lined lots of retail shops and small businesses—including a pawnshop or two—but not the major big boxes like Target or The Home Depot, that generally signaled the nearby presence of green, manicured neighborhoods with moderate to high THIs (total household incomes).

That didn't matter to me, although maybe it should have. I just wanted to be a grown-up and thought buying a house was the responsible thing to do. Also, it was close to my church, which was the only consistent support system I had in Atlanta.

"Why do you live over *there*?" asked several of my White colleagues, who either lived in upper middle-class neighborhoods or in palatial tennis and golf communities.

"Well, it's close to my church. I'm active there." That was generally my pat reply. Since most of the people I worked with claimed to be Christians, I figured that might soften their hard looks. It didn't.

"But isn't there a lot of crime over there?" they persisted. "I mean, it used to be thriving once, but...it transitioned."

"Crime is everywhere." *Jerks.* I was just a junior consultant and wasn't making the money they made—whatever exorbitant amount that was to afford their lifestyle. Didn't they know I was young, single, and just getting started?

"Oh...yeah, that's true," was their only reply, but by then I was already tarnished in their eyes. It wasn't long before a buzz seemed to circulate among a few higher-ups in the company.

"So, exactly *what side* of that street do you live on?" asked one of the senior officers at a department-wide retreat in the presence of some of my peers. A rise of heat filled me, and at that moment, I felt dirty and poor. Living outside their normalcy made me unfamiliar, too different, and one more reason for them to alienate me.

Like a wave of the hands, their words penetrated into my psyche like a Jedi mind trick. At home, I buried my head in my hands, crushed that my biggest asset had become my biggest embarrassment.

Did this company really want my diversity? Because the more different I was, the more isolated I felt.

I slowly descended into a dark space of constantly questioning myself, dissecting my every move, word, and decision pertaining to my work and life. Many nights I went to bed, sometimes in tears, wondering, *Does this company approve of me?*

Once, Josh hosted a potluck dinner at his kingly estate on a hill for the team and their wives. I didn't have time to cook—many of my teammates' wives didn't work outside the home, and thus, had the flexibility to prepare something—so I bought a broccoli and cheese casserole dish from a local chain in my neighborhood. People seemed oddly curious which restaurant I got it from. As we prepared our plates, I tasted from mostly everyone's dish. When the party was over and it was time to leave, I glanced over at the kitchen island in dismay. Most of the dishes were ravaged, except for one. My broccoli and cheese casserole looked untouched minus the corner dent from my scoop and perhaps a half-scoop by someone else. My spirit broke. Nobody wanted my casserole.

"See y'all tomorrow!" I forced a smile with my loaded dish in hand.

My heart grew heavy on the drive back home.

I had sunk into a pit filled with uncertainty. I still hung on to the belief that I worked for a great company, but every day was a fight. I needed an escape.

Home was my first escape, where I always felt safe. It yielded me the space and permission to dream and imagine, which I did almost every night in the stillness before I closed my eyes. Even though I had no plans of leaving the company—I determined to tough it out—I still dreamed.

One of my favorite biblical stories was about Joseph. Like me, he was a dreamer—with a big mouth. His mouth got him in trouble with those closest to him; he was thrown into a pit and sold into slavery. Joseph was tested, falsely accused, and could have given up on life, but he held onto what he could control and put it to use—his faith, his gift (he could interpret dreams), his work ethic, and his integrity. He eventually went from being the least of men to one of the greatest of men. Like a seed that's planted in dark soil, Joseph's life was also very dark before he towered in the light. And he grew where he was planted.

Joseph's story gave me hope to hang in there. The company wasn't perfect, but I knew it was still a good company. I believed I was there for a reason.

"I'm not giving up!" I spoke aloud into the darkness of my bedroom one night, floating in the imagination of my future self in bold, beautiful brilliance. One day, I would grow to become her and shine.

But I was stuck in the darkness figuring out how to survive in the company where I was planted. Everything about me seemed to be evaluated, commented on, and critiqued—my spunky eyeglasses, my hair, my shoes and accessories, and of course, where I lived. Even my single status became a constant topic of conversation. Once, I got hurled into human resources with a libelous, anonymous fax to the company that I was gay and molested children at my church. My church validated my character with a letter to the company after I found out it was authored by a jealous, troubled church member. *Damn.*

Church. That was my only other escape. The soulful praise and biblical teaching inside that old brick building with a simple steeple renewed my spirit like a slice of warm, soft bread every Sunday. One, I was around people who looked like me. Two, the people made me feel safe. Three, feeling safe made me want to engage and serve more. And four, engaging and serving more made me feel valued.

I led the drama ministry there. It was where I stayed connected to my truest dream. I wasn't the best performer, though. In fact, acting really wasn't my gift. It was the effect I had on people through my skits, plays, and even the *sound* of my voice. I beamed like the rays of the sun. The words that flowed through me moved people toward a greater good.

That's when I knew my life was really meant for a stage. Not for acting, though, but for *impacting*. That was where my genius lay.

I wanted to feel as valued at the company as I did at church. There were no handouts, though. The only way my situation would change was if *I* changed.

So, *I* had to be content with God being my only audience. *I* had to focus and maximize on the things only I could control— my faith, my attitude, and my learning and development. Like Joseph, I had to be my own champion.

I recalled Josh's advice to me in my office: "Just keep learning." Funny, I remembered Evelyn Matthews, the eloquent brown sage at the bank, who told me something similar in her office when I was having problems with Jed. I could hear Evelyn's charge now: *Learn from them. Learn everything you can!*

So, I did, or tried to. I started with my money. There was clearly a gap between where I was and where the men were. They lived the American dream. I believed I could live it, too. So many of my teammates openly talked about the financial markets, buying and selling homes, and investing during our team meetings. Class was in session. I listened and took notes.

Then, I read financial books on my own—Larry Burkett, Suze Orman, Dave Ramsey, and so many others—to better understand the language of money. I repeatedly listened to audiobooks like Napoleon Hill's *Think and Grow Rich*.

Then one day, my mindset started to shift. I began to think in terms of net worth rather than set a savings goal. My house was no longer an embarrassment, but rather future rental property. I met with financial planners and opened investment accounts, making itty-bitty contributions each month with pay raises and other bonuses. I cut down on spending, kept Sassy around, and didn't even look at new furniture for the house because I knew that eventually I would move. I also paid tithes at the church. Over time, I saw a shift in my net worth. It was growing.

At work, I cross-traveled with people outside of my immediate team to shadow them. I read the books they read, studied their style in consulting meetings, watched how they prepared, paid attention to what their follow-up looked like, and how they made decisions. Everyone had a different approach to their work. But the best lesson I gleaned had nothing to do with their technique. It had to do with their heart: *Serve people first, then success will follow.*

Even church became a source of learning and development. It honed my leadership skills with the drama ministry and gave me practice speaking publicly. I gradually began to soften my heart toward people, especially my team.

"Give grace to others because you'll need it one day yourself," my pastor would teach.

That's when I chose to forgive those slight offenses from my teammates and believe they were there to help me grow. Regardless of how many times they pissed me off, I still searched for the good in them.

And then one day, it happened—a breakthrough, a "coming out" moment.

It was my first stage with the company.

Loud, throaty growls of motorcycles filled the parking lot. Media flashed their cameras at some of Atlanta's "who's who." High school bands and cheerleaders electrified the atmosphere.

Executive corporate brass was everywhere, including the company founder himself. The air crackled with anticipation.

It was a milestone marker, a major grand opening establishment for the company that landed in a market I consulted. The mayor of Atlanta, other dignitaries, company executives, and a host of company staff and fans buzzed throughout the grounds for this ribbon-cutting ceremony.

Since I had oversight responsibility as the market consultant, I had an opportunity to give remarks in front of this local, "star-studded" crowd of more than two hundred people. It didn't matter that my speaking part was bit-sized, that I only extended the welcome and led the pledge of allegiance. The occasion was not about me and I was no star. I just wanted the opportunity to be *seen*, to let the company—and my team—see *me* in a new light.

There weren't many times in the past, if any, where a Black woman spoke in public on this level as a representative of the company. To me, it was a big deal.

I bubbled with excitement, feeling like I held a winning lottery ticket. At home, before the event, I stood in front of the mirror and rehearsed my welcome a thousand times, even though it wasn't more than four or five sentences. I never liked speaking from notes.

I made sure I looked the part. I chose my best black suit and complemented it with a chunky pearl necklace. My hair was tightly pulled back into a high thick bun. Nails were freshly manicured, and my rich red lips made my pearly whites shine even brighter. Grandma Ethel and Grandma Mattie would have been proud.

When I arrived onsite, Josh and several of my teammates were already there, chatting. Their eyes lit up when they saw me.

"Look at you!" T.J. said. Ever since the fall planning retreat in North Georgia a year ago, he looked out for me like a big brother and always made himself available. I believed he genuinely rooted for my success. "You look great!"

"There she is!" I didn't have to look behind me to know that comforting voice, a sound that always made me exhale. It was Josh, who walked toward me with welcoming eyes. "This is a big moment. You ready?"

"Yes, I am!" I exclaimed. I looked up at him, grinning. "I'm going to make you proud!"

I didn't know why I couldn't be more executive-like and stoic with Josh. He simply made me soft and giddy. He unlocked something inside me, a feeling of freedom to be...just *me*. I had never felt this sort of freedom with Jed.

"You already do. I know you'll do great." Josh gave my shoulder a gentle squeeze then walked away to talk to the company officers who'd come to support the event.

It was time.

When I took the podium, I felt so centered. My voice behind the microphone carried volume, filling the tent with articulate precision and a captivating warmth. My brief remarks were flawless, and the entire event went off without a hitch. Of course, everyone else who spoke shined, too.

For the first time, I actually felt like I had scored with my team, who didn't hesitate to pour in their compliments.

"You have so much presence! I'm so proud of you," commented T.J., who gave me a high five.

I blushed.

"You know—most people get nervous or overwhelmed at big events. But you," Duke paused, searching for the right words. His eyes studied me as if I were revealed to him for the first time. "Well...you rise to the occasion."

"Thank you, Duke." I said sweetly, lowering my head. I almost wanted to give him a hug. "That means a lot coming from you."

Even Jackson, whose rigid demeanor often signaled the sound of trombones, had something positive to say. "People light up when you speak," he declared, and then favored me with a nod. "Good job."

That evening, I bounced around the house like a kid on a sugar high. I'd finally did something that made the team acknowledge my value. I was seen, even though it was only for a brief moment.

It was the best day I ever had with that company in my first two years working there.

Shortly before my thirtieth birthday, I achieved my goal of being a land owner. I moved out of the eastside, converting my house into rental property just as I had envisioned. I then moved to an "approved" side of town in northwest Atlanta. I found a Victorian-inspired, fixer-upper kind of home that needed a lot of love to be restored to its original charm. Frankly, it was more of a money pit. But I saw its potential and closed on the house anyway...my second house! Now, I had *two* properties!

A few months later, after five full years of employment with the company, Josh recognized me as a new senior business consultant in front of the entire department (finally, I crossed over into six figures of income!). Except for one teammate, whose eyes froze on me with a stare that yelled "token," mostly everyone else on the team seemed genuinely happy for me.

Not long after my promotion, however, Josh called me into his corner sunlit office to share news that shattered my world.

"The company is restructuring, and I am leading a new team," he said, searching my face. I wanted it to be a joke, but there was no humor in his eyes.

My heart sank. I couldn't move. My hero, the one sure person in the organization I knew was on my side, would be exposing me into the hands of another. I knew this day was bound to come. He couldn't be my boss forever.

"Well, say something," he gently probed, but I was paralyzed at that moment.

I really didn't know what to say, except the obvious.

"Who's going to be my new group leader?" My words came out slowly. I knew I looked like a child who'd lost her best friend. I didn't hide my disappointment. All I could think about was self-preservation.

I listened as Josh outlined the restructuring of the department and how the consulting teams would realign. T.J. would be promoted and become my new boss.

I exhaled.

T.J. was humble and, like Josh, was well-liked by the company. He was also always very encouraging to me. Thank God I didn't have to start the cycle of building a new relationship all over again with someone I didn't know.

"Can I still come to you? You know, for advice? To talk?" My voice was heavy. "Will that be okay?"

"Of course, you can! Hey, I'm not going anywhere!"

Josh stood and wrapped one of his long arms around my shoulders like a father consoling his daughter and gave me a gentle, brief squeeze. Water welled in my eyes.

After our meeting, I immediately dashed towards the ladies' room, where I collapsed inside the empty stall. I was lost. It was another bathroom moment.

Josh was an encourager whose empathy was as high as the moon. No one in the company believed in me the way he did. I became fiercely loyal to him. His unique ability to shepherd and build people filled a hole I didn't even know was there, something deep and barren inside my soul. It ached to be separated from him.

Josh showed me what it looked like to lead with heart. I aspired to be that leader to others the way he had been to me—one who was fair, encouraging, and able to see the unique talents in people. A leader who always learned.

One thing was for sure, I had never met anyone like him. After that day, my interactions with him diminished like the sands of time. People often changed when they got a little taste of power. I only prayed that wouldn't be the case with T.J. I liked him as my peer. But would he champion me the way Josh did?

I didn't know. That's why I had to become my own champion first.

Now, more than ever.

CHAPTER 5

Broaden Your Exposure

There was no need for me to be afraid, but I was. I clutched my pillow in the cool, quiet darkness of my "prayer closet" while curling my body on the soft carpeted floor. My mouth watered with metallic bitterness as my feet rubbed together in constant motion. I struggled whether or not to take an international trip to Africa.

It was early spring in 2007. I had never flown across the pond. The fright of an airplane splashing into the deep rolls of the Atlantic Ocean panicked me into a cold sweat. There would be a layover at Heathrow Airport on the way to Lusaka, Zambia, the destination of my first international mission trip sponsored by the company.

I scoured the world map to even find where Zambia was. At first, I leapt at the chance to join a team to teach young, emerging leaders on servant leadership in some exotic land. That was, until the naysayers injected fear.

"Make sure you can outrun at least one person," muttered a wary sixty-year-old colleague, whose idea of "missions" was going to the exotic green tropics and savage beauty of Costa Rica. "If you want to do *that* kind of mission, just go to downtown Atlanta."

I had to admit, the idea of going to a primitive, unfamiliar land sounded, at first, wildly adventurous. However, I did have visions of some of the more dangerous lions, leopards, and other giant, wild beasts and predators, as well.

More well-meaning skeptics chimed in with their arrogant admonitions.

"Don't drink the water!" declared one. Well, actually, that *was* sound advice.

"Humph! I'd never do *those* kinds of missions," spouted another, a suburban housewife who always stuck her nose in the air. Her voice dripped with disdain. Sometimes, she joined her husband, my coworker, on international missions. "We just stick to Western Europe."

"Keep your windows closed. A monkey might get in," whispered a third.

And then, the most severe comment spooked me like a paranormal haunting.

"Make sure at least one person on your team has your blood type, you know, in case you need to go to the hospital. They all have AIDS over there...."

The idea of taking such a big leap into the unknown was terrifying. But something had "called out" to me at a company-wide meeting several months ago about *this* particular trip. It was an escape, a chance to leave myself—to get out of my head—and step into something new. I had always wanted to experience the world, especially the "motherland." And the company, if I chose to go, would underwrite most of the trip. It was a great opportunity.

But there, alone in my closet, I grappled with the fear of being attacked, abducted, or contracting something.

"Oh, you'll be fine, Juliet," chuckled Will one day after telling him I was having second thoughts about going to Zambia. He was a company colleague and the point person for the trip. He shook his head, then patted my back like a warm uncle. His belly jiggled when I told him what some of the people in the office had said to me. International missions were nothing new to him. "Be sure to check off all the items on the preparation checklist," Will said in a hoarse, smoky voice like that of a football coach. "You have your passport already, right? Get all your shots, and bring meds for traveler's diarrhea and malaria. Pack light and bring insect repellent like you're going camping. Then, you're all set."

Will made it sound easy, but camping was for White people. I didn't know about that life.

Little did I know what awaited me in Zambia.

"Welcome to Lusaka!"

We had just walked outside of baggage claim with our luggage. Our Zambian host, Alfred, took measured steps towards the American team with outstretched arms and a giant smile. His clothes draped loosely over his lithe body, boasting the golden-orange hues of an African sunset. But the best part were his shoes—thong sandals strapped with coarse beige-like hair, possibly cut from a lion's mane.

Alfred turned to me after shaking Will's hands. "It is a pleasure, Juliet. I am happy that you are here." His deep voice boomed with fluid choppiness.

I was in Africa!

There, on Zambian soil, I paused for a second while the men took the luggage. I filled my nostrils with the dry heated air, expecting to feel some sense of nostalgia, some leap in my heart, or some blow of the arid wind that carried a faint whisper of, "This is home."

Instead, I felt nothing—except a little fatigue and stickiness from my seventeen-hour flight.

Lusaka's airport wasn't anything I had imagined, even though I had no idea what to expect. Rusted crisscross rails framed the façade, giving it a closed, cagey appearance. But inside was completely different. Big, square-tiled flooring glistened throughout the terminal, and there were several ticketing kiosks. Airline employees were officially uniformed, and postured just like those who worked in America. Even going through customs was seamless. Flashing our navy-blue passports made our passage effortless.

I made my way to the dusty white Volkswagen minivan where Alfred, Will, and others were loading the luggage. There, beside the van, stood an athletic blonde woman who waved at me.

"Juliet! Hi, I'm Ursula!" She took my hand and gave it a gentle squeeze.

"So good to finally meet you!" I said, studying her.

Ursula's voice and appearance were unequally yoked. Her voice was as light as a feather, yet she stood before me now, erect and equal-footed like a Norse shield maiden. She had a strong jaw and sun-kissed hair that she wore into a high-braided pony-tail. Her eyes sparkled like green crystals.

"Don't let the soft voice fool you," Will told me weeks before our departure to Zambia. We had several conference calls with Ursula, who lived in London. Her ministry was supported by my company's foundation. Will and I, along with one other colleague, volunteered to represent our company on this mission to teach servant leadership to young, up-and-coming leaders in Zambia. Will led the American team, but the overall mission was Ursula's gig. "She can be hard as nails."

The men continued loading the minivan with the luggage while Ursula and I climbed inside it.

"How was your trip?" she asked in her light British lilt. I leaned forward and noticed sparkling embers in those green translucent eyes.

"Oh! Very long!" I said with a laugh. "It's my first time traveling overseas. So glad we're here, finally!"

Ursula nodded with understanding. She made a living traveling all over the world teaching leadership disciplines in underdeveloped economies. I imagined her home looked like the United Nations. The exuberance of taking that first long journey, the newness of the experience, probably wore off on her a long time ago.

"Glad you came," she said.

The men finished loading the minivan and hopped inside.

"Let's go!" Alfred said.

And so, the adventure began.

I woke up the next morning in the bottom bunk of the bedroom, checking my arms and legs for mosquito bites. The bedroom window remained open because there was no air conditioning in the house, but thankfully it was cool at night—and not a monkey in sight.

There was nothing elaborate about the bedroom. Thin, anemic-gray carpet covered the creaking floor. A bold blue brushed the walls. Across the room from me was Ursula, sleeping soundly in her twin bed against the sole window. Her golden hair spilled off the pillow.

The guesthouse, overall, was small by American standards, though perhaps generous by Zambia's. It only allowed for two square bedrooms—one for me and Ursula and the other for Will and his roommate—and just one tight bathroom we all had to share. The kitchen was as long as two sticks, barely fitting an old refrigerator, stove, and sink. A single couch and love seat were squeezed in the living room.

I jumped out of bed and shot to the bathroom, on a mission to take my shower first. We were informed there had been issues with the plumbing and that the hot water—and water in general—could run out. I was prepared, though. I brought wipes and packed as if I were going camping, as Will had instructed. I used bottled water to brush my teeth.

Almost two hours later, Alfred picked us up in his Volkswagen and drove us to the venue where we would be teaching. We pulled into the dirt driveway of the Salvation Army, a facility that looked like it hadn't been touched in many years. There were long, single-story stretches of khaki buildings—the main hall, dormitories, and office space—with tiled roofing and powdered-blue window frames and doors.

"Oh! Look at the little baby!" Ursula pointed to a small box house a stone's throw across the front entrance of the facility. I saw him, or *her*. A little bald crawler in brightly patterned top, probably no more than a year old, nibbled on some small yellow fruit while sitting on the threshold of the opened front door.

I hopped out of the minivan and scanned the premises for stray animals. There were no monkeys, hyenas, or lions lurking around. All those naysayers back home in Atlanta, influenced by the media, assumed the country would be some barbaric land inhabited by wild animals and humans half-clothed in beads and straw. They were grossly mistaken. No, it wasn't posh like Atlanta's Buckhead, but here in Lusaka, the country's capital, it was just modest, basic living from what I could tell. And so far, it was safe.

As we neared the front door, my feet stopped. My ears perked to a faint rushing sound, the rich harmonies of a cappella voices. I looked over to Ursula, whose face lit with excitement.

"Let's go see!" she said like an eager explorer.

We walked inside the main hall, and there they were, the students, lean and gaunt, who colored the room in their African garb. Their dark skin shone like satin, as if the louder they sang, the more they illuminated.

Something moved in the air, a force I couldn't see. It tugged on something deep inside me. I stood like a statue in the back of the room against the wood-paneled walls, watching. They were beautiful, rich, and guttural voices that didn't require any musical instruments, only hands that clapped with precision and authority. Heads tilted back as they bellowed with closed eyes and sweat glistening on their foreheads. This was not mere singing. This was a heart's beating, a fervent petition, and a joyful cry. My body stirred as tiny hairs stood on my arms.

God was here.

I traveled to Zambia with the intent to teach. Somehow, I became the student.

There were roughly thirty young leaders in the class, mostly men in their mid-twenties, who represented some of the brightest minds in Lusaka. A few also traveled from Zimbabwe and South Africa. Many of them had aspirations to lead a church, but there were some who aspired to grow a business or lead in government ministry. I noticed only three women in the class, and they were silent as mice.

Tradition was king. It covered the room like a shroud. The women sat together as if by instinct, in the back or off to the side, while many of the men moved around the room to engage with each other. As students introduced themselves to the American team, many shared the meaning of their names. And as they shook our hands, they positioned their left hand underneath their right elbow. The manner of their speaking was more proper than many Americans I knew. Their formality was just as refreshing and respectful as it was rigid.

After the morning session, which consisted of a devotion, quiet time, and two presentations on leadership, the class moved into the fellowship hall for lunch. The table spread showcased an appointment of Zambian culinary tradition—rice, fruits, spiced vegetables, whole fish, and some type of stew. There was also a very thick porridge, called *nshima*, a Zambian staple made from finely ground white corn. It reminded me of grits. My eyes glued to the way the students ate their food with their fingers. Plastic utensils were provided for us Americans.

As the cooks replenished the trays of food, I noticed a bundled lump attached to one of the cooks—a chunky little baby boy with a dollop of hair snuggly wrapped on his mother's back. There were no daycares on this side of Lusaka, I presumed.

Like a magnet, I left my lunch to follow the cook into the kitchen. My heart jumped as I approached the little baby. His cheeks were like two fluffy muffins dipped in milk chocolate. I so badly wanted to take a bite.

"Oh, hi!" I said sheepishly to the cook. "Your baby, what's his name?"

She stopped and met me with an easy smile. "Songwe," she said, gently. "He's nine months."

"Songwe," I said, singing his name. I sighed with a sharp maternal fondness over this little boy. "Oh, please, may I hold him?"

Songwe's mother untied her wrap and presented me with her baby in what seemed like one quick continuous swoop. I took Songwe and held him up to my eyes. He looked at me with a deep, penetrating gaze that offered the dignity and quiet command of a tribal chief. Then I squeezed him against my chest and melted into his soft, plump innocence. I was in love.

Songwe didn't cry. He didn't smile, either. He held his head back while exploring me with puzzled eyes that spoke, "Who *is* this light brown woman with a strange voice?" His little fingers found my shoulder-length hair and lightly pulled. I planted kisses all over his round mocha face while his young, doting mother looked upon me with a smile that stretched from ear to ear.

"You don't have any children?" she asked, tilting her head incredulously, even though it was spoken more like a statement. I guess it was obvious that I didn't, based on the way I tightly cradled Songwe. At thirty-two, I wasn't even married. In her culture, I was considered an old maid.

"No, ma'am. But one day, I hope." I released a nervous laugh and gave the African baby another squeeze. "What is your name?"

"Ruth," she replied.

"I'm Juliet." I returned Ruth's wide smile and handed her son back to her. "Thank you for letting me hold him. So adorable!"

I left the kitchen to join the others in the fellowship hall, but my thoughts remained in the kitchen with that nine-month-old boy.

Evening came. The crisp Zambian twilight sky canvassed the elaborate universe with shades of a dark bluish purple, boasting ubiquitous stars that sparkled like diamonds. Inside, the room was dim and faintly lit by low-wattage bulbs. It was like looking through a dark screen. Since there was no air conditioning, the opened windows settled the room, diluting the musky air.

Ursula shone like a torch as she delivered the evening devotion. All the students leaned in with intense curiosity. The room stilled to hear her tweet-like voice.

"Leaders develop in isolation." She paused to pierce into the eyes of the young African hopefuls. "God trains you in His secret places."

My heart fluttered as if those words were meant for me.

"For the next few days, while you're here—and there is no distraction—expect God to enlarge your *tent*." Ursula smiled as she scanned the faces. "Your tent is your heart. God will increase the tent of your heart, to receive more knowledge, to receive more of Him."

Heads gently nodded. I jotted notes in my own journal. Ursula's words, though few, were like choice morsels.

"And as you grow in your leadership journey, there *will* be fire. But fire refines. It takes pressure to bring out the best in you, to crack and release what's inside you." Every eye remained fixed on the blonde warrior princess who towered among the Africans seated around her. Even in the room's dimness, her eyes shone like pools of moonlight. "So, enjoy the fire...while your character is being developed."

Soft-spoken Ursula, from London, had taken me to school.

Later that night, I mulled over her words in silence from my bed as I stared into blackness.

There was no television for me to watch. I didn't have an international plan on my Blackberry to connect with family. And, of course, there was no Wi-Fi or access to the internet in the humble guesthouse. The noise of American culture, even the tone of American superiority that inherently haloed me, began melting on the Zambian soil until all that was left were my thoughts.

It was as if I were being stripped and hidden like a seed covered in dirt. No one could find me here except God...in Zambia, one of God's secret places.

Tomorrow, it was my turn.

My hands shook a little. My eyes darted around the room like a trapped bird seeking escape. Even though I was a leader, I had never taught anyone how to become one. This was a different type of stage. There were no spotlights, no script, no props, no makeup. Just pure, raw teaching in a classroom where I was the foreigner.

Somehow, I felt out of my league.

"Don't worry!" Will told me earlier that morning. "Speak from your heart. Teach from your experience." Even with his encouragement, my heart still raced with nervous uncertainty.

The young Zambians began the morning session with a praise song that went on for days. I didn't mind, though. I just wish we could have sat down after the fifth chorus. But their music was something different. It set a mood and stirred the soul like the burning of incense. And it did relax me, just a little.

As the students finally took their seats, I inhaled a deep breath and walked to the front of the room, hoping I might sound like an authority on leadership.

"What does it mean to serve?" I began.

My eyes caught several blank expressions looking back at me. A few curious glances darted into empty spaces.

"Serving implies a duty, an action—helping others for the benefit of others, and to achieve a goal."

The room did not move.

"Leadership is for everyone, including women." I looked at Will a couple of times for reassurance. He nodded often to let me know I was doing okay. I caught the eyes of the three women in the room. Hints of a smile formed on their lips. One of them offered a nod.

"And the best leaders are those who serve."

Then came the awkward silence. Several men looked down, while others wore puzzled expressions on their faces. None of them nodded their heads.

"Leadership is *serving*?" One of the male students raised his eyebrows. "What do you mean? Like cleaning? Doing the work of servants?"

"No, not necessarily," I replied, clearing my throat. My forehead moistened. "You serve through being an example...through humility and with character. That doesn't mean you do other people's jobs. But sometimes, it means walking alongside them. Servant leaders aren't dictators. They care about people and build them up—both men...*and* women."

Finally, there was a stir. I was rattling their proud, patriarchal tradition.

One after another, voices chimed in, followed by an eruption of raised hands. There were rumblings across the room as they tried to comprehend the concept of servant leadership, and even more, to get comfortable with the idea of women in leadership.

"But women...well, here, we don't have women leading—eh, not in our church!"

Several men shook their heads, as if the thought repulsed them.

A groundswell of murmurs shook the classroom. My armpits developed a mist of perspiration as questions flew at me. This topic of women in leading roles, or just servant leadership in general, was like walking on hot coals. The three women in the classroom shrank into the shadows. Ursula said nothing, but surveyed the room like a hawk while scribbling notes.

I glanced over at Will for his reaction, or perhaps to ask for help. I couldn't think of words to say. Given I was in a room full of junior patriarchs steeped in their tradition, I thought it would be helpful if he contributed a comment. He must have seen the pleading in my eyes.

"You have to choose," Will finally spoke up, calmly, like a wise chief, "what kind of leader you want to be—especially as men of faith—and what you believe to be right...despite your culture. Should your beliefs submit to your culture, or should your culture submit to your beliefs?" His words were like putting balm on a sore wound, and a thoughtful stillness breezed through the room again.

There was no applause, no standing ovation when I dismissed the class for a break. None of the men came up to me afterward to say "good job" or "thank you" or "you're right" about this or that. My head hung low as I walked outside the building for some fresh air.

"Thank you for saying what you said. That women can also lead." A soft hand touched my arm. I turned around to see one of the female students, Aneni. Her gaze oozed on me like warm molten chocolate. There was a rich goodness there. She was one of the students who'd traveled from Zimbabwe to attend the leadership retreat. "It's hard for women in our culture."

I found us a bench and asked her to sit with me. Many of the students strolled outside for their break, talking and laughing in huddles of three and four. A few men held hands while going for a walk, a common gesture in this culture as a fond and platonic display of friendship.

"What's it like for you? For women in your culture?" I asked.

Aneni paused and looked out into the distance in deep reflection. "You're expected to marry around or before the age of twenty-five. Many women are abused, sexually, even in the church. Even when it's not their fault, women are still shamed." She possessed the rich and resonate tenor of an orator, but with notes of sadness.

I saw in her a profile of steely determination mixed with quiet longing for freedom. And just then, I remembered. It was as if I were a teenager all over again, in my own house, treading in a system of punishment and control. The conditioning, sermonizing, and infliction of guilt...the flashbacks of my youth made my cheeks flush with the memory of many stings.

"What do you want to do?" I touched Aneni's hand. "When you leave Zambia, this retreat, and go home, what do you want to do? What's your vision?"

She searched her own thoughts before looking at me. "I want to empower women. I want to start a non-profit organization for women who have been raped and abused."

I squeezed Aneni's hand and looked firmly into her eyes. "Yes, Aneni. You can."

A glow lit up her eyes. She stood, nodded, and walked toward the dormitory.

Later that evening, in bed when the lights were out, I pondered this universal attack on women. I thought it was bad enough in corporate America. But it was just as bad, if not worse, in less developed countries with patriarchal cultures, where traditions not only kept women in mental bondage, but also inflicted shame. Religious folk were the worst. It just didn't seem fair. Sometimes I even wondered, *Did God hate women?*

Ursula whispered to me across the room, breaking my thoughts. "You did good, Juliet. You got lots of questions today. That means you made them think."

I was glad that I got her stamp of approval, but I still had a nagging sense of uneasiness that I could have done better. I drew the thin sheets to my neck, cowering in my bed, thinking the young men might have thrown rotten tomatoes at me if they could.

"Thanks." My mind still burned, replaying every word a thousand times. There was a first time for everything. Thankfully, my trial run was here in Zambia—far away from home—and not at the company, where I would surely be judged.

"Yes, it *was* good. Believe me. But rest now. Tomorrow will be a long day. Get ready."

"Ready for what?" I asked, confused. My biological clock was off with the six-hour time zone change. I didn't even know what day it was, let alone the agenda for tomorrow.

Even with the lights out, Ursula's sharp green eyes cut through the darkness.

"Tomorrow we go to the slums."

I sat frozen in the kitchen, hunched over with no words inside me. My eyes found a square in the faded linoleum floor and didn't move. It was lunchtime, but there was nothing inside me to feed.

Ruth handed me a cup of hot tea and gently squeezed my shoulder. Songwe hunted for his next adventure, crawling on the porch just outside the opened kitchen door but within earshot of his mother's voice. The other kitchen cook refreshed the table with more food for the students, who feasted as if this were their last meal.

"I've never seen poverty like this." My eyes never left the floor. I didn't even know how I managed to find and force those words out of my mouth.

Tears gushed down my face. Ruth abruptly left the kitchen to grab some tissues from a nearby restroom.

A heavy weight descended on me and stayed there. It was like being stuck in a bad dream, except it wasn't a dream. This was *real*. In that chair, my mind replayed the horror of the Zambian slums.

As soon as the early sun rose and shimmered in the sky that morning, the American team departed for the slums with Alfred. Ursula, somehow struck with a stomach bug overnight, stayed behind at the guesthouse.

On the way to the slums, we first stopped by a brown, remote housing complex to visit a family Alfred knew. We walked down a row of units and paused. Before my eyes was the sight of a limp body lying on the ground, covered by a thin, soiled blanket.

She couldn't have been more than nineteen. The girl was frail, with small scattered lesions on her arms. Her coarse, untamed woolly hair trapped days, if not weeks, of sand and dirt. Mosquitoes dominated her powdered brown face. Her exhausted eyes stared past me, and if they hadn't blinked, I would have thought she was dead, but she wasn't.

"She has AIDS," Alfred whispered as we all walked closer to the young woman. "She got it from her boyfriend, someone much older."

We all stopped at the mat to acknowledge her. No one touched her, but we made light conversation. Or, we tried. Her lips barely moved, and only brief whispers escaped her, but she managed to give us a faint smile.

My chest throbbed with pity. Will's face turned pale as milk.

There was no access to health care and no drugstore at every corner for this young woman like there would be in Atlanta. Her life hung by a thread through the prayers of others or, possibly, a witch doctor.

Alfred motioned his head toward what appeared to be a dark hole. "Let's go inside. We can speak to her mother."

The unit was one flat floor with three functional spaces. As we walked inside, we immediately stepped into a squat living area that contained a ripped skeletal couch, an antenna television, and a stained mattress that reeked of dried sweat and old urine. One dirty white doll head and other incomplete toys scattered along the floor like debris. Three steps to the left was a single stove, and behind the pocket living area was a partial wall that hid space for, perhaps, another mattress. There was hardly any light in the unit except for the natural brightness that spilled through the front entrance and one single window. Behind me, I thought the wall moved until I stepped closer and noticed multiple trails of bugs and insects pinned to the wall. I wrinkled my nose as my arms peppered with goose bumps. I held my breath for as long as I could and didn't take another step.

We greeted the woman who mothered her fading daughter stretched outside on the ground for light and fresh air. She was about 5'3" and quite sturdy. Her lips pressed into a thin line that pronounced her long jawbone. She leveled her head as she looked unwaveringly at me and Will, the Americans. The woman couldn't have been more than forty years old, and though the whites of her eyes looked worn and waxy, they still exuded strength.

I didn't know how Alfred knew her, and I didn't ask. She didn't say much to us and kept her hands by her side except to hurriedly wave them goodbye.

My shoulders tensed at the thought that maybe she caught how my eyes widened with horror at her living conditions. I remembered how lowly and offended I had felt when my company colleagues turned their noses up at the location of my first house. The last thing I wanted was to carry the same cold air of American pride and privilege.

"How many people have AIDS here?" I asked Alfred after we loaded back into the minivan.

"About eleven to fifteen percent. But those are *reported* cases." His voice trailed off, hinting at dismay or perhaps embarrassment. "It's sad."

As Alfred drove toward the business district, a modest skyline came into view. More cars flooded the streets. Faded billboards popped up advertising vehicles, phones, and beauty products. A pastel-colored Coca-Cola billboard had taken a beating from too many years under a hot sun. *Coke is everywhere*, I mused.

Everything I'd witnessed in Zambia so far, including this view of the city, seemed dusty and dated and trailed at least a quarter of a century behind the Western world. Still, the familiarity of civilization—tall buildings, banks, traffic, noise, even the sight of a Coke—fueled me as if I were back home in Atlanta again.

Alfred drove through the market, where multitudes of vibrantly dressed pedestrians lined the sidewalks to purchase goods from outdoor vendors. And then I saw something spectacular—women who balanced large baskets of produce on their heads while walking.

As we moved away from the city, we passed by a woman on the street who stood with a baby wrapped to her chest. One of her tits poked out in broad daylight while her baby sucked on the other one. And there it struck me, as I marveled, that even in material lack, creation still equips us with what we need to live and survive.

While Alfred continued for miles down an endless rural road, my eyes grew heavy. We had departed the guesthouse not even two hours ago, and already I was tired. My body began to sink into darkness until the minivan knocked me out of my slumber. Alfred turned off the road and onto the gritty unevenness of gravel. I immediately sat up, held onto my seat belt, and looked out the window as he drove into a massive compound that almost made me shriek.

We had entered the slums.

There was a taste in the air. An odorous stench crept through the vents, a pungent tang of days' old blood and rotten flesh. The foulness clawed at my throat. It reminded me of the sharp bite of chitterlings—or *chitlins*, pig intestines that smelled like cooked feces, food once eaten by slaves but still cooked in some Black southern homes today. I immediately covered my mouth to contain my breakfast. And then I saw it. The head of a goat, masked by flies, hung by its horns with dark, bloodied eyeballs that peeked through half-closed lids. A butcher stand selling meats displayed a decapitated animal like a trophy along with other parts like legs and organs. There was no refrigeration, no packaging, and no health code, just a slaughtered animal chopped into pieces and sold out in the open.

Alfred forged through unpaved, uneven dirt. The minivan bounced every ten seconds as he drove over small holes and sharp bumps.

I couldn't breathe. There were endless clusters of shed homes, as far as the eyes could see, made of cinder blocks, cardboard, tin roofing, and bedsheets for doors. Outdoor laundry lines scattered throughout the compound, waving clothes and sheets in the air. A few women cooked outdoors using a small pot atop a few small sticks of fire. Scores of dusty Black children ran in circles, kicking a half-deflated soccer ball with their little feet. Some wore only stained underwear. Others were draped in generations of hand-me-downs, grimy mixed-matched T-shirts and shorts. There were one or two toddlers who wore nothing at all. Despite their being scantily clad, the brightness in their eyes did not diminish. They played in their squalor and squealed as if they were in Disneyland.

As the children saw Will's face in the minivan, they ran toward us waving, smiling, and posing. To them, a White face in the slums signaled charity, sustenance, and rescue; a delivery of boxes and bags of toiletries, clothes, toothbrushes, and other supplies. But we had none to give.

"Where are the men?" Will asked Alfred. I noticed it, too. I saw lots of women and children, but very few men.

"They leave. Some find jobs. Many die from disease. A few join gangs. The average life expectancy for men—here, in these slums—is thirty-five years." Alfred knew so much about life here.

"My church comes here often. We do lots of charity work—it's important to me."

"Do people ever make it out of here," I inquired, "and live successful lives?"

He grinned. "Yes, they can. They do. I speak from experience. I grew up right here."

My mouth dropped. Alfred was so polished, so...clean.

"That's why I come back. To help others. I mentor young boys." He glanced at me from his rearview mirror. His eyes twinkled, seemingly amused at my stunned reaction—and, perhaps, proud of his miraculous accomplishment.

"*How*? How did you get out? Of *here*?"

"When I was a boy, someone mentored me."

Quietly, I nodded. Will did, too.

Then the minivan stopped. Alfred pointed toward a round rusted flat covering on the ground about the circumference of a large trampoline. "That's their well, where they get their water for everything—to bathe, drink, cook. It's not clean, but it's all they have."

My head squeezed tightly, as if it were stuck inside a medieval torture device. It was too much optical noise—mounds of scrap and debris covered the compound like a hideous quilted blanket. There was no order, no uniformity, no cleanliness—it was an undeveloped society inflicted with chaos and a lack of governance. This was a land without laws, a family without a father, and a community without leadership.

It was a world I didn't understand, a world in the deep south of hell.

How could *this* be anyone's normal?

My body shivered. I leaned back in my seat and rubbed my eyes, trying to cancel out the horrific images of poverty that, by now, depleted all of my energy until my insides felt as if there was nothing there.

"It's very hard. We need help." Ruth's soft voice brought me back to the present. She handed me a tissue.

"I've never seen anything like this before...in my life...poverty like this." I spoke in between gulps of tears. My head still throbbed from the minivan's bouncing on the uneven roads. "I didn't know."

Ruth pulled up a chair beside me. I rested my head on her shoulder, broken, in a river of tears as I kept repeating myself like a malfunctioned robot. "I didn't know."

But there *was* one thing I knew. God had enlarged *my tent*.

I would never be the same again.

There was a sad soreness in me. It was like leaving summer youth camp, but stronger. I probably dropped a tear or two on the way to Lusaka's airport. The rich, soulful songs of the students still rippled inside me like soft waves.

When I returned to Atlanta, I was as tall as the trees. There was a weight in my eyes.

I became mindful of the little things now, like how often I kept the water running when I brushed my teeth, how often I let the water run before I stepped inside the shower, how often I threw away food, why I needed a four-bedroom house as a single woman, and how many cable channels I paid for but never watched. I lived in extreme abundance, and yet I was extremely wasteful.

When I got off the plane at Hartsfield-Jackson Atlanta International Airport, there were only two things I desired. First, I longed for a hot shower, which I realized now was a luxury. And after my shower, I wanted to fold myself into the downy sheets of my plush pillow-top king-sized bed—another luxury.

But really, only one thing mattered now.

At home, I studied myself in the bathroom mirror. "What now?" I asked myself. *To whom much is given, much is required*, I thought. "What can I do with what I have?" All that mattered in that moment was that *I* wanted to matter. I wanted to make a positive impact on the lives of others, now more than ever.

I felt as if God had pulled me up out of toxic American culture to see another world. The experience of traveling internationally to a land much different than my own deeply changed me. What used to be important—like wanting to be accepted as "one of the boys" at work or striving for that next promotion—now seemed small. The type of house, cars, and brand of clothes I aspired to have now all seemed so meaningless. The people I knew and worked with who seemingly didn't value or appreciate my presence became as insignificant as a puff of air. Even religion, as an institution, seemed small—God was bigger than any building, bigger than any man...even bigger than any book.

"But what do I do? *How* do I matter?" I asked aloud, looking up at the ceiling in my shower. There was no audible reply, just the therapeutic pounding of endless hot shower water. "What exactly is my role in this world?"

I kept asking, but didn't have the answer.

I dried myself, draped on clean clothes, dove into my American abundant bed, and within minutes, drifted into a deep sleep.

For two weeks, the weight in my chest never went away. During that time, I kept up with a few of the Zambian students through

Facebook and email, though the communication waned after the first week. I still hungered to do more with my life and sought to figure out my "new" assignment, purpose, or role. And then one day, an unexpected request came to me on a Sunday afternoon after church service.

"Juliet, will you write us a play? For our twenty-fifth church anniversary? We want to celebrate in a big way! Maybe even take it to a public venue." My pastor's wife, Sister Bev, was always full of ideas. She was the heart of the church and possessed a flair so contagious that every young woman wanted to be her daughter. She also carried such an air of regal authority that no one ever dared to tell her no.

"A play? Hmm..." I didn't know if I would have the time. I still led the drama ministry, but writing a play was a lot of work. Doing skits didn't require writing, but a full play? It had been three years since the last full two-act play I wrote. It *was* a good play—the church had loved it!

"You would have lots of help—a team. We've never had a person to write a play like you. Please?" Sister Bev flashed her signature grin, that confident gap in her white even teeth that projected her strength and appeal, which she wielded on cue to make people gush and fall into her charms. My eyes lit up with her words of flattery. She was good at stroking egos to get what she wanted.

"Oh...*alright*! I'll do it." I didn't consider the turnaround time to write, build a production team, cast actors, schedule rehearsals, among many other factors. The anniversary celebration was five months away. I spoke too soon.

Later that Sunday evening, I tossed and turned in my bed, racking my brain for an idea. What would I write about? I needed to submit an idea and an outline to the church office soon. But my mind was still stuck with the memories of Zambia.

"That's it!" I bolted up in my bed and switched on the table light. I could write a story inspired by my experiences in Zambia—but set in Atlanta, in the bowels of the city, where there existed an American version of the slums.

"The Mission…" I spoke the title of the play into the atmosphere.

Yes, *The Mission*.

I reached for my journal and filled up pages with story ideas. *A young woman says "yes" to venture into the inner city to serve the residents while all of her comfortable and privileged friends abandon her except one. Together, they touch and inspire the lives of a prostitute and a homeless man and get them off the streets and into a better life.*

The pastor's office loved the idea.

There I was, excited, to be back on a stage. This time, we would be performing to a sold-out crowd of approximately 320 people in the main stage of the Woodruff Arts Center's 14th Street Playhouse in downtown Atlanta—a community theatre on steroids.

The Mission title flashed in bright lights on the marquee of the playhouse. I just stood there, lost in thoughts. My dreams, though quiet, still had a heartbeat and remained as loyal and as close to me as my next breath. There, in front of the marquee, my mind scrolled back to almost ten years ago when I stepped onto that small stage inside a barren theatre, performing my heart out to eight kids and a teacher.

And now this. A sold-out audience. A play I wrote and directed. All because I was obedient to an internal urging, a call, to get out of my own day-to-day comforts to try something new and scary that would serve others and develop me in the process. This was growth.

When the curtains went down, there was a standing ovation.

Many of my company colleagues, including T.J., were there.

"Juliet, I don't know what my expectations were about the play. But I got to tell you—I laughed, I cried. The play was amazing!" He left me a voice message after seeing the play. I saved his message for weeks.

There were other notes and messages from my colleagues, who all gave me major "creds."

One of my White male colleagues left me a tearful message about how the play struck a deep chord with him. "I saw myself in one of the characters," he said. "Thank you. That play...it really affected me...."

The word was out. Even one of the company's vice presidents introduced me to one of his friends, the president of an Atlanta-based bible college, to work with him on a playwriting opportunity for his school. Ironically, my outside pursuits fueled my internal credibility.

The following year, in 2008, T.J. promoted me to management consultant.

In his company remarks, he called me the "resident Shakespeare." This was a huge promotion—it was like making partner in a firm. I was escalated to an executive compensation plan, which made my income soar every year based on company profits. I made the big bucks now.

And yet, there were still a few faces in the department that seemed puzzled. One of my male peers came up to me one day, boldly asking how I had the time to write plays.

"Where do you find the time to play *golf?*" I retorted.

"It just seems, well, wow..." He never did finish his sentence.

"You spend your time playing golf. I spend my time writing plays."

He walked away quietly.

Ten years. I made it *ten* years working for a company that also worked for me. There were people who didn't think I would make it that long, let alone be promoted to the level of management consultant. But I did it—and with more than just a big smile.

Inside the main floor of the company building, my eyes scanned the packed, lofty atrium. Hundreds of mostly vanilla faces filled the folding chairs on the floor. Others lined the stair rails, overlooking the stage. The company founder and CEO, along with his cabinet of vice presidents, stood off to the side of the platform. It was the company's staff recognition ceremony honoring fifth, tenth, twentieth, *even* thirtieth anniversaries.

And the company had asked *me* to be its speaker.

I began by thanking the founder for providing opportunities for all staff to grow and develop as leaders inside and outside the organization. Then, I got real.

"In my travels, I have realized that despite who we are, how we're raised, our educational backgrounds, or the color of our skin, that we are *still* more alike than we are different."

The building became still. People held their breath. Eyes fixed on me with a look of uncertainty. I definitely had their attention.

"And that applies to all of us in this company, too. We may not have all gotten our start working together at the same job as teenagers, we may not have all attended the same schools or churches or even live in the same neighborhood in the same area of Atlanta...but we all love this company."

The room exhaled.

"We all share the same needs of being seen and treated with honor, dignity, and respect. We all desire to be great in what we do and to be recognized for it. We all support the core values of this company and are members of 'the family' regardless of how we came into this organization. And we *all* want to matter...."

There was generous applause after my speech. People flocked to me, gave me enthusiastic hugs. They all shared their thoughts.

"Thank you, Juliet," said one staff member, a Black woman, who was also celebrating ten years with the company. "I truly felt you represented me."

"When you talk, you make me want to hear more," said T.J., a few minutes later. He beamed like a big brother.

"That was great...and I could hear a little bit of a challenge for us all," said a graying White woman, a higher-up who was known to tout her vice president title throughout the company. There were other vice presidents, too, who reached out to me with positive notes on my speech.

It was a coming-of-age moment. The once ponytailed young adult who trembled in the bathroom stall when a man intended to exclude her from a team bonding trip stood tall today, as a Black woman who spoke truth to an entire organization about how we all share the same human needs to belong, be seen, be successful, and be significant.

Finally, I had broken into the light. My name began to grow in the company.

And so did my voice.

CHAPTER 6

Be Open to New Opportunities

The sharp buzz of my cell phone pulled me out of a deep sleep. I jerked upright, although my eyes were still too heavy to fully open. My left arm stretched toward the nightstand, blindly groping for my phone.

"Hello?" I croaked.

"Juliet, I'm so sorry to wake you. I have bad news." Thomas, my realtor, whose office managed my rental property, spoke in a tone low and somber, like that of a graveyard preacher.

In the stillness of the night, I braced myself on the bed, clutching a pillow. One eyelid parted just enough to peek through a haze of tousled hair toward the dim glow of the bedside clock. It was almost two o'clock in the morning. "What is it? What happened?" My voice was barely above a whisper.

"Your house—well, it caught on fire. It's pretty bad."

Both eyes flew open and darted into the darkness, which lightened just enough for the furniture silhouettes to appear.

My hand tightened on my phone while I held my breath, hoping his next words would not crack with devastation of the unimaginable—a body being burned alive.

"The tenants are okay, thank God," Thomas said. "They had a small baby. No one was injured."

"Ah!" I plopped my arm onto the bed, relieved, though scant moisture sprang on my body. "Thank God. So, what...what happened? The fire, how did it start? Was there an electrical issue? Did something go wrong in the house?"

"No, no. It was the tenants. *Their* fault. They left the stove on...with a pan of hot grease."

My face twisted. I felt like someone who'd been duped by a Halloween prank. I had no words and didn't know whether to cuss or cry.

"You'll need to call your insurance company first thing tomorrow. The tenants have already evacuated. I'm so sorry this happened to your property. Your insurance should handle it. Just call them and make a claim."

I shut my eyes, swallowed all the air in the room, then exhaled. Life was a blur that early in the morning. Thick fog clouded my mind between work—and now *school*, which I had in a few hours. In the fall 2009, a year after my big promotion to management consultant, I enrolled in the Executive MBA program at the Terry College of Business at the University of Georgia. I was only a few months into the program, though with the long nights of study and conference calls with classmates, it already felt like a year.

"Okay," my voice stumbled with grogginess. "Thanks, Thomas, for letting me know." I returned the phone to the nightstand and rolled over in my bed. My rental property was the least of my worries at the moment. As long as the tenants were unharmed, I could sleep.

Insurance would take care of the rest.

But then, and not long after, winter came. And after the fire came the flood.

It was an unusually hard winter in early 2010 for Atlanta, where winters were mild and rarely dipped below freezing for any extended period of time. Not that year. Ice slicked the streets overnight in bone-freezing temperatures where there had been rain. Weather forecasters warned to keep the faucets dripping overnight, which I did prior to my departure for a company-wide meeting in Washington, DC.

Still, the fangs of winter bit deep into the bathroom pipes of my home in northwest Atlanta. Water gushed over two days from my master bathroom on the top floor, flooding my bedroom and penetrating the floors underneath it. Both my kitchen and basement ceilings collapsed, which triggered the house alarm. All of this inconvenient news came to me in a phone call from my security company while I was hundreds of miles away at a company seminar I couldn't leave.

"We sent the police, then a fire truck to your house. The firemen entered through your back door," the security operator told me. Her monotone voice sounded bored, flat, and more like a robot than human as she shared the status of my home. "They broke in and turned your water off."

I squeezed my eyes, hunched over on the bench in the spa's locker room. At that moment, I was wrapped in a plush white terry-cloth robe, preparing for an evening massage at the Gaylord Resort and Convention Center, which stood on the shores of the Potomac River. Both elbows were on my knees, my left hand pressing the phone into my ear while my right hand cupped my bent head. My only wish then was to be small enough to crawl inside the glossy wooden locker and hide there.

When I ended the call, I just held my cell phone in my hand, staring at it, as if expecting some serendipitous buzz from someone, anyone, who could help and tell me that everything would be okay. I had no immediate emergency contact in Atlanta I could call except for an elderly next-door neighbor and a distant, aloof aunt who could do with or without me.

The massage therapist guided me into the dark room where I settled myself, belly down, onto the massage table. Soft music filled the room with recorder-like sounds backed by air and water, the sort of calm that would have drifted anyone into a dream-like world but had little effect on me. My body stiffened with thoughts of my house under siege by water; on top of that, I had to give a school presentation on business financial risk days after I returned to Atlanta.

"You're very tense," the massage therapist spoke in a low, hushed voice. She elbowed her way into the sinews of my back and shoulders, smoothing out the knots scattered around my upper body.

A week later, I had a meeting with T.J. in his office. His pale blue eyes were wide with compassion, especially when I told him I had been living in a hotel while my home was being dehumidified.

"Just tell me what to do," he said, with empathy. His heart was in every word.

"I don't know, T.J.," I murmured, shaking my head, my eyes on the carpeted floor. "But, thanks. Thanks for caring."

"Hang in there. Please tell me anything, absolutely *anything*, you need," he persisted. His words were a gift, like a single ray of sunlight that broke through a heavy cloud.

For several weeks thereafter, I traveled across the country for work, toting pounds of books the size of encyclopedias inside my luggage, attending classes on the weekends and forging through a few sleepless nights—while *homeless*. Needles poked around my head every night as my weekly routine seeped the life out of me—airports, work meetings, general contractors, classes, classmate conference calls, endless emails, constant study, hotels.

I was almost headed for a crash until the day I mustered the courage to call my executive coach, Victoria. She was the psychologist assigned to me by the university.

"I'm just afraid," I told her, while on the road one dark, dreary day in West Virginia on a work trip. I unleashed a stream of violent sobs that had been bottled up for far too long. "Afraid of being a failure. I feel so alone." I finally let it all out, all my frustrations and my fears, tears freely falling down my face. I was driving and the roads were all a blur. I slowed down as the angry blaring of car horns passed by me. "I have exams coming up...finance and accounting...I don't think I'll pass, Victoria. I have so much on me now! I'm scared—what if they kick me out?"

"Juliet," Victoria interrupted. "I want you to pull over, find somewhere to park...now!" Her voice had the careful firmness of a mother. "Right now, you are in the fire."

Fire. The word struck me like a thunderbolt. Ursula's opening message to students in Zambia suddenly flashed back at me.

"I want you to hang up and call Rich," Victoria continued. Rich Daniels was the Executive MBA Program Director. "Tell Rich *everything*."

"But—I think Rich is in China right now." My voice trembled like a young, feeble teenager whose heart just got broken by a high school crush.

"It doesn't matter. He has a phone. Pull yourself together and call him. If you don't get him, leave a message. He will call you back."

"Okay," I said, sniffling. "I will. I'll call him now." I hung up.

Like an obedient child, I pulled over in the ghostly parking lot of a worn retail store, where months-old promotional posters were stuck on grimy windows. I fumbled through my purse for the red and black business card with an arch logo as wipers noisily scrubbed across my windshield.

To my surprise, Rich answered on the second ring. I told him everything, and tears began to gush out of me all over again.

"Oh, Juliet," Rich said in a voice filled with compassion. It shocked me. His personality was normally distant, and he possessed an odd touch of nervous energy. "I'm really sorry to hear that. But don't you worry, we can get you help. We have tutors if you need it. And you always have your teammates."

"I'm so afraid you might kick me out of the program."

"No, no...we won't kick you out. A lot of our MBA students experience life issues. We understand that and support them as best we can. There's a reason we have a high graduation rate. We want all of our students to succeed."

Rich was right. Life happened to other students in the program, too. There was a classmate on the verge of a divorce, another who got laid off work, and a couple of women with unexpected pregnancies. One or two students dropped out altogether. Everyone had their stories.

Suddenly, the world around me seemed to brighten a bit. My sobbing gradually slowed down and eventually stopped.

"Just take a deep breath," Rich continued, "You'll be fine. And keep coming to class."

"Okay. Thank you, Rich. Thank you so much." There, in the parking lot, a weight was lifted off me. It stopped raining. As the sun parted the heavy clouds and stroked my face, there was a slight lift to my spirit, and at that moment, I knew I was going to be okay.

I passed my exams—barely. But I still passed. I stayed in the program, continued going to class, and asked for help when I needed it. I got acclimated to the rigors of life–work–school, and eventually what at first seemed hard wasn't hard anymore. It was normal.

The following year, T.J. rolled out some unwelcome news to our team.

"There's going to be another organizational restructuring," he said. All eyes were glued on him as he scanned the room. The entire team of consultants waited expectantly on his next words. I held my breath. "I'm going to be leading a different team, and Kyle is going to become your new group leader."

The room shuffled a bit. A few heads quietly nodded, but there was no outburst of applause. Kyle was known for having a good relationship with the department vice president. He possessed the flair of a campus frat boy who breezed throughout the office halls with a casual smirk. A few years ago, I remembered approaching him once to request a meeting with him on a certain matter, and his flat response to me was "More power to you."

Then, he kept on walking as my eyes followed his back, speechless.

Kyle, I pondered, in curious dismay. He was another man being promoted to group leader. After more than ten years, I'd seen the company grow in diversity. Yet men, especially White men, were still promoted more often in senior management and higher roles than any other group of people, followed by White women; a truth for many companies in corporate America.

My corporate eyes lost the fresh dew of bliss and reckoned with a reality that was so apparent. Kyle, and many others like him, possessed something intangible that gave him an edge. I doubted it was his intelligence, hard work, or whiteness alone, even though he possessed all three. Kyle had amazing access. He was mentored by executives who looked like him, was often handpicked for special teams with executive leaders, was regularly spotted eating lunch with them, or casually lingered outside their office doors. Kyle's access haloed him.

The access was fostered outside of work from the many stories I had heard over the years. T.J. and Josh had the same access, whether it came through living on the same side of town or in the same subdivision, attending the same church, having the same college affinity, connecting through the same friends, and in some cases, benefitting from marriage and nepotism. Access was a key to visibility, familiarity, and likeability with those in power. Those who had access seemed to have a more promising career path over those who didn't, who only yearned to be acknowledged, mentored, and tapped for higher leadership based on real talent, merit, and years of service.

Be grateful flickered in my mind like a neon sign, admonishing words I could hear my elders say. And I was. I worked for a good company that paid its people well. Not everybody got an invite to this party. Still, there was no crime in my aspiring to grow, to ascend to the next level, whatever that might be.

Enjoy the fire, I sighed, recollecting Ursula's words from her opening devotion in Zambia, *while your character is being developed*. Her terse words carried the weight of mountains and never left me.

No, Ursula, I thought. *I don't want to!*

In a trance, I sat locked in the stillness of my car. As I sat, comforted by the heated seat that cradled me, a shroud of nervous uncertainty loomed. I was scheduled to meet with my group leader, Kyle, with no clue as to why he wanted to see me.

I racked my brain, retracing my steps. Had I done something wrong?

No, I thought. My life was finally back on cruise control. It had been a year since I graduated from my MBA program, my rental property was fully restored with new tenants, and the flooding of my house had led to a massive remodeling journey that brought some order and upgraded beauty to my life. I even led an international mission project to Durban, South Africa and participated on several others. I endured and finally made it out of the fire, one that burned every remnant left of "Juliet, the girl" to reveal the whole of "Juliet, the woman."

Yet there I was, unsettled, in the company parking lot, watching the early sun stretch its rays through timbers that partially veiled the office building. Droves of lively people stepped through the glass doors wearing smiles as plastic as their name badges. I took a deep breath before peeling myself from the car to join them.

I walked into Kyle's minimalistic office, an enclosed corner cubicle brushed in eggshell and taupe tones with a sliding glass door. With strong sensor florescent lighting and a little greenery, his office space seemed barely touched. It sparkled like it was brand new. A single eight-by-ten rustic picture frame of his wife and kids, all coordinated in white tops and beige bottoms standing on a beach, was displayed on his desk next to his office lamp. A closed laptop rested on the side of his desk.

Kyle was lean and fresh-faced with strong, pointed features. Thick eyebrows hovered over his hazel-green eyes and chiseled chin. Every strand of his brown hair was in place. He was definitely "in" based on his looks alone.

"So, how are you?" He leaned back in his chair, crossing his legs like a Southern aristocrat. He distanced himself a foot or two behind his desk, far enough for me to see a perfect crease in his silk pants. He tilted his head and gave me that annoying squinted eye look, as if to suggest he knew me better than anyone.

"Great." I nodded with a closed smile. I offered no other words, which prompted Kyle to get straight to the point.

"Well...I know there's been some struggle working with some of the clients. I've seen you get emotional and frustrated."

I flinched and sat up straight in my chair. My brows bunched together, wondering where Kyle was going. Several months ago, he traveled with me while I was still in the throes of school and house restoration, and true, I had gotten frustrated with some of the men who turned cold on me because of hard decisions I had made in their markets—decisions supported by Kyle and the rest of the team.

My throat tightened while my hands gripped the armrests. "Frustrated? Well, sure, I was under a lot of stress, Kyle...you know, with school—"

"You can't use school as an excuse, Juliet." He cut me off. "You can also be very direct. You underestimate how strong your presence is."

I was silent. *Direct? Strong presence?* He said that like it was a bad thing.

Kyle's gaze steadied on me as if I had misbehaved. "You're so independent, like you don't need me or anybody." He uncrossed his legs and scooted his chair closer to the desk, leaning forward and resting his arms on the desk. "This role...is it the right fit for you?" he asked, his voice barely above a whisper.

My eyes narrowed as one who discovers a bitter truth: that a friend has become a foe. All of a sudden, the room got warm. My armpits tingled. I couldn't find the words, couldn't even fake a smile. My back tightened as I glared at Kyle and wondered if he questioned the fit of *men* whenever they got frustrated and emotional. I'd witnessed one or two in particular who were known crybabies—yet, they were described as having "a big heart." But here in this moment, my "emotional" was code for *unfit* for the job. I knew not to question Kyle on this. Otherwise, he might construe me as combative and confirm me as the stereotypical angry Black woman.

Or, maybe he already had.

I took several long deep breaths to calm my racing heart. Maybe his question was fair, I thought, even though I resented it. After all, I liked my work but didn't actually *love* it.

"What else could you see yourself doing?" Kyle asked, breaking my reverie. I was reluctant with my response. Instead, I looked upon the calm taupe wall, pondering his question.

I sighed, resigned, and was slow and tentative with my words. "I don't think—well, maybe, the role I really want, the role for me, hasn't been created yet." I paused while Kyle continued to listen. "I see myself in a public-facing role, I think, but not PR. A company ambassador—like a spokesperson, of sorts."

Kyle didn't react. He acknowledged my dream with a slow nod. "Okay," he said, and kept nodding, as if he might see it, too. However, there was a problem. No appointed role or department with this job description actually existed at the company. "Well, let's keep talking about it."

I offered Kyle a half smile and quietly walked out of his office.

Later that night, I tossed and turned in my bed, replaying every word in my meeting with him. There was still a residue of awkwardness, that feeling of uncertainty met with a slight bruise to my ego. Kyle hadn't been my group leader for a year yet, and I wasn't altogether sure if he was really trying to support me or push me off the team.

My mind swirled with the dozen years of my employment at this company; neither Josh nor T.J. ever questioned my ability to do my job. Instead, they recognized and elevated me in my consulting role, and even appointed me to mentor one of the newer consultants in the department.

But Kyle's words frustrated me: *Is this the right fit for you?*

Fit...what did *that* really mean?

Most of the clients I worked with were White men, many of whom carried rifles and drove pickup trucks. For many of them, I was the first woman and person of color they had ever worked with, and while many of them were nice, others openly snarked upon me with hard eyes because my role gave me a measure of influence over their opportunities.

My role. It offered me so much treasure—tuition reimbursement for school, the ability to pay for expensive home remodeling upgrades, the means to vacation to any country I wanted, and the luxury to go on $3,000 shopping sprees at the drop of a dime. For the first time, I became a symbol of success in my family, who respected my accomplishments as much as they did my sister's.

Random thoughts of the worst kind burned in my mind of what might happen if all of that success was stripped away. Would I still matter? Or were these golden handcuffs holding me back from pursuing a bigger dream that still called out to me?

My mind often warred between my dream and my livelihood. One offered a sense of mental freedom, whereas the other offered financial peace. I longed for them to be one and the same, but I didn't know if my dreams belonged in this company—or now, if

I even did. New opportunities were created all the time, but the people who normally snagged them were White and/or male.

I was worn out from the everyday fight of trying to fit in into an environment that seemingly favored the elevation of Whiteness and familiarity more often than not. "Window dressing" opportunities were important and encouraging and easily afforded to people who looked like me, such as appearing on diversity brochures, annual reports, and videos. But none of those had any permanence nor carried the weight and authority of a high office. No one in the C-suite was a Black woman.

Once, Duke, my teammate, implied in so many words that I was just an optical illusion. Several years ago, he had asked me to participate in an internal company training video. "We need to show diversity," he said flatly.

On a more recent occasion, I brought a company leader, at her request, to my undergraduate institution, Spelman College, to meet a few of the chief administrators there.

"We're looking to broaden our diversity and want to build relationships with HBCUs, especially Spelman," my company leader said in an even, cool tone. The way she fidgeted in her seat suggested she wasn't used to being the only White person in a room. "I've lived in Atlanta my whole life but have never been *here* before. Your students...well, they are so *impressive!*"

The proud, stoic college officials nodded their heads in agreement, though their eyes were guarded and expressionless. They studied this woman I had brought to their table, patiently, as she continued speaking.

"We need strong Black women to lead. At our company, we just don't have *any.*"

It was like a stone had smacked me. I caught the eyes of one of the college administrators, who glanced in my direction before looking back at my company leader. Her eyes became like glass.

My honey-brown face reddened with a warm flush. They didn't know how much the company paid me, though money seemed so trivial in that moment. I dropped my head, seething, fiddling with my fingers as I listened to my company leader rattle on about *her* position. I regretted bringing her to my beloved alma mater.

Reminiscing on my humiliation deflated my spirit. At home in bed, I stared at the white stenciled ceiling trying to remove the power from that painful memory. My eyes were dark and heavy. I had invested so much into myself—going back to school, developing my community leadership, and broadening my cultural awareness through my international travels—but all my growth needed someplace to go where it could be utilized, valued, and appreciated.

It was as if I stood limp at a crossroads like a wounded soldier, tired—tired of the fight, tired of having to be superhuman when the majority group could get away with just being average.

I squeezed my eyes and pulled the sheets over my head so hard I could have ripped them. My body writhed inside the darkness, and though my lips wrenched apart, there was no immediate scream; only a continuous string of sharp, raspy gasps.

"I'm s-so tired!" I hollered in between breaths. My mouth found the words while my fists balled and beat the bed. "I'm tired of the struggle, tired of always fighting. Please take this weight, this burden, away from me! Give me your plan and purpose for my life. It's got to be better than anything I can do on my own. Open the right doors and close the right doors. I want *your* best for my life. *Please*, oh, God! Give it to me!"

Amen.

"Guess what! There may be an opportunity for you," Kyle began. Today was Monday, roughly three weeks since my last meeting with him, and there was unusual positive energy in his voice. "One of the VPs saw you on stage at one of our company awards. He heard you speak, and he wants to talk to you about a possible opportunity."

"Oh, yeah?" I perked up in my chair, flattered to be noticed. "What kind of opportunity?"

"Tours. He wants to talk to you about leading company tours."

"*Tours?*" My face shriveled in disbelief. I was ready to walk out of Kyle's office. "He wants *me* to give tours?"

"No, no. Not give tours. Build it. Lead it. Market it. This could be a really good opportunity. The executive office has a big vision behind starting company-wide tours. You would be creating something new. It could go as far as you take it. And you would work closely with executive leadership."

I responded with a side-tilt of my head and gave my best Black version of a *Chile, please* look. Kyle was spinning now, exaggerating this so-called opportunity, "putting twenty on ten."

"You said you liked to speak. Wanted to be a spokesperson... well, you'd be involved in telling the brand story to a lot of people, to groups, to different organizations," he said.

I wasn't sold. The only people who really took tours were... well, tourists—like school kids on a field trip or senior citizens in an assisted living home who needed something to do. This felt like multiple levels below my pay grade.

"What if I want to stay where I am?" My pride kicked in. I felt the rise, like a volcano about to erupt. I didn't completely trust Kyle, who sat before me now so broad and formidable. He seemed eager to get me off his team and, perhaps, needed me to own it like it was my idea.

His face colored a shade of pink as he firmly pressed his lips. "What you're doing now, this role, it's not working for you. I know you're not happy. It is what it is."

"Well, I've been in this role for a long time, and none of my previous leaders felt this way! Everyone struggles with something!" I snapped back.

So much of this role was based on relationships, how much other people liked you. On scorecards, my quantitative results were great. My market performance was among the top in a few categories just a year ago. But the department yielded to "trust" surveys, which, I thought, was odd as a measure of objective performance. People instinctively trusted what was familiar to them. It takes time, years even, to build trust in any relationship. My "trust" results were up and down, though good enough overall, before school, but had fallen to average or below average for the two years I had studied for my MBA.

She's a truth-teller. She's direct. She's brutally honest. She's not in the right seat on the bus, some of the anonymous clients had responded.

"This is a non-confrontational culture," Kyle retorted in a condescending tone. "Josh and T.J. should have told you. That was the right thing to do." He rocked back in his office chair, looking under his eyes at me.

I clenched my fists and was ready to thump him now. He crossed the line throwing shade at the good leaders in the company who preceded him, men who gave me a chance and were fair and supportive—men I had *access* to.

"Okay," Kyle relaxed and tried to level the conversation, "you can say no. But let's at least just meet with the group leader in charge of the work, you and me. Let's hear what he has to say."

I squinted my eyes but acquiesced. Something about the opportunity felt soft...and small.

Later that week, Kyle and I walked together to a small conference room to meet the group leader for this potential opportunity. He stood, and his eyes smiled at me. With my high heels, I stood about an inch taller than him. He drew me in right away.

"You're good on a stage, Juliet. I remembered hearing once that you wrote and directed plays at the 14th Street Playhouse, right?"

I favored the man with a smile, impressed that someone I didn't know well knew something about me. "Thank you. I wrote that play several years ago." I glanced over at Kyle, who sat straight in his chair and didn't move. He was just the broker.

"Well, you're a really good communicator, and because of your role as a consultant, I know you have leadership ability." Then he leaned forward as he described the vision behind the company tours.

There would be some travel, but not nearly as much as the weekly travel I was required to do in my consulting role, and so maybe I would have more of a social life. *Check*. I would get to utilize more of my strengths and build upon a new area of business within the company. *Check*. But did this opportunity possess any real gravitas? *Hmm*. I struggled with this one. The opportunity seemed better suited for a young emerging leader, or an employee reaching retirement age as the sun began to set on his or her career.

"This role can expand," he continued. "There may be projects we want you to lead, maybe even help develop a speaker's bureau for the company...but that may come much later. Build the tour first, hire a team and market it to the public—and grow it. Give it some thought. I'd like you to consider it, but if you don't want it, I need to recruit someone outside the organization."

For the next few days and nights, I laid restless in my bed, mulling over this decision. Maybe, just maybe, this proposition was an answer to a prayer and one step closer to my dream. If I stayed in my current role, there would be no more upward mobility left for me. *Not with Kyle*, I was certain.

"Let me not despise small beginnings," I whispered, prostrated, in my prayer closet one night. "If this is the path You have for me, then please give me peace."

The peace never came, not the kind of calm that felt like cool, clean air blowing in my body after a yoga class. This was an edge-of-the-cliff moment. The stakes were high and adrenaline coursed through my veins. I looked down and out into an infinite terrain of possibilities, where only my mindset could determine whether I succeeded or failed. My chest drummed as I contemplated the jump, and I realized then it was never peace that I needed. It was faith.

I said yes.

I gazed outside the jet window and caught my reflection in the pane. I had taken another leap as a Black woman.

I chopped off my hair.

No more did I straighten it with relaxers and harsh chemicals that often burned my scalp. That was the old me, thinking that my natural hair wasn't beautiful enough. But it was, and my fingers loved its strong, velvety texture that was styled into a pixie cut. *This* was me.

And as I nestled into the soft leather and strapped on my seat belt, I pinched myself to make sure I wasn't dreaming. All the seats, maybe twelve in total, were wide, as wide as the seats in business class on a commercial flight, and they faced each other in clusters. There was a long, leather bench on one side. Glossy wood grain trimmed the inner walls, the long tray tables, the galley's cabinets, and the lavatory door. The beige carpet was brushed thoroughly, like long thick hair. All the furniture in the cabin was either cream, beige, or brown—elegant, but not overly stuffy.

Sitting across the aisle from me was the senior vice president of the company. He hadn't removed yet his stiff wool felt Homburg hat that posed its signature feather on the side. He looked intensely busy shuffling a file of papers. Behind me were a few other executives who came along for the ride. I just smiled as I relaxed into my chair and reclined it a bit. I had never traveled on a private corporate jet and thought to myself, *If only my grandmothers could see me now!*

Months after I said yes to my new opportunity, I took on a special assignment to collaborate with the executive office and assisted in the orchestration of a chain-wide, thirteen-city tour to roll out a new company mission statement. It was a new stage, the kind of opportunity that offered me supporting speaking roles. My internal visibility soared and gave me regular access to the executive office, where I learned more about the company from a panoramic view.

"You are a thought leader, Juliet," the senior vice president told me from time to time. "And I like hearing you speak; you're captivating. You have a lot of leadership capacity."

I was never prouder to be a part of the company as I flashed the senior vice president my biggest smile.

"I am your biggest cheerleader," he often encouraged me.

And so, there I was, at the top of my career, close to my dream space and with access to influential people. This was genuine access that didn't come from "sameness" or familiarity. Rather, it was the result of tapping into my gift, of leading from my area of strength.

I remembered, once, my pastor quoting a proverb, "Your gifts make room for you and put you in the presence of important people. When you operate in your gifts, you don't need to play politics, promote yourself, or jockey for position. People will find you because of your gift, because you have something they need."

How true, as I recalled, once again, the story of Joseph, one of my favorite biblical characters. It was Joseph's gift that took him out of prison and brought him into the presence of Pharaoh, who later elevated him to the second highest position in the land. But it only happened after Joseph had endured his fire. The sweetest juice often poured from a crushed spirit.

I wouldn't have had this opportunity if I'd held on to my pride and stayed in the department with Kyle, who later got removed from the team. *Hmm...*

As the corporate jet lifted into the sky, I closed my eyes in gratitude, loving the woman who was gradually emerging from inside of me.

CHAPTER 7

Remember Your Gift

There I was, basking in the bright lights on a glistening wooden stage, cloaked in my black robe with my eyes aglow and a smile growing of its own accord. I looked inside my black folder for the one-hundredth time to make sure my speech was there, then gazed into a blanket of dark gray as a blur of students, the Class of 2015 from Georgia Military College – Fairburn Campus, walked down the aisle inside the Martin Luther King, Jr. International Chapel in the Morehouse College campus. As my ears filled with the all-too-familiar "Pomp and Circumstance," those long notes that powered my nostalgia with fond, sweeping memories of ending one chapter and beginning another, I couldn't help but stand on stage with humble reverence, inhaling the spirits of giants, past and present, who at one time were there, sitting in that same audience or standing on this same stage where my feet were planted now. All that was troublesome or mundane or trivial was muted because the only thing that mattered was today. I was in my element, my space. I was *being* Juliet; a voice that encouraged and exhorted with words and stories. It was here, with a speech in my hand, where it felt like a crown had been placed on my head, where the world just made sense to me and life no longer seemed like an impossible maze. Money and status didn't matter; only the words I would soon sow into these young souls were important, the words that I wove like fabric and rehearsed multiple times to make perfect. I did it all, with little effort, because those words were already a part of me. The stage lights that showered me, the microphone that would soon fill the hallowed chapel with my voice of hope and possibility—all made me warm inside with a joyful vigor like that of a child. I knew then with unequivocal confidence that *this* was what God had in mind when He created me.

Standing to my right was the grinning campus president of Georgia Military College – Fairburn Campus, a man with whom I served alongside on the board of directors for a chamber of commerce. He had approached me at a chamber luncheon several weeks ago about speaking to his graduating seniors.

"You want *me*?" I asked, dumbfounded. I was already honored at the luncheon that day with the "Board Member of the Year" award from the chamber. *Now this?* I was over the moon!

"Yes, you! You're such a great speaker and so accomplished— so well-put together. You're just the type of professional woman I want the students to see. I know it's short notice, but the school superintendent who was supposed to speak got another job opportunity and relocated. I need someone to speak, and I want you!" His eyes were clear and wide and soft with so much regard for me until I felt tall like a giant.

My lips parted in a huge smile. But the words didn't come out of me right away. Instead, I felt a slow burn spread through my chest, a subtle flag of warning, although it had nothing to do with the campus president. I had been getting noticed a lot lately in the community, the kind of visibility that made a few of my company colleagues give me hard looks. They were probably asking themselves, *How is she getting all these opportunities?* But my presence was bigger than my title; my talent larger than my sandbox. Here I was, a manager, being tapped for a speaking opportunity traditionally marked for people with higher titles or bigger platforms, and I knew this new spotlight, though honorable, would only make me a bigger target among the jealous.

"She'll do it!" Beside me, another fellow board member, Denise, interrupted my silence to answer his question. "Yes, Juliet will be your speaker!" She spoke emphatically as a girlfriend who had my back. And then she looked at me, shrugging her shoulders and as she said innocently, "Well, you told me you liked to speak."

The president turned to Denise, whom I forgot was even there until she inserted herself into the conversation, then looked back at me with raised eyebrows and a chuckle.

I shook myself. "How many people do you anticipate at the graduation? And where will it be?" I asked.

"About 1,500, including the parents and teachers. It'll be at the MLK Chapel. An evening ceremony. Will you do it?" He pressed his hands together in quick back-and-forth motions, like a fervent prayer.

"Yes, okay, yes!" I laughed exuberantly with no more afterthought of the repercussions. "I would be honored." I couldn't believe this opportunity had fallen into my lap, a chance to be the commencement speaker of a military college. Denise was beaming.

But I should have believed in myself. I shouldn't have had doubts. My gifts were making room for me, gifts that were there all along inside me, ever since I was a child.

And I should have remembered this truth. One night when I was eight years old, an image still so vividly and indelibly imprinted in my mind, my hand had instinctively reached for a pencil and a notebook like candy. I had plopped on the forest-green linoleum floor in the den of my house and, out of nowhere, I just simply started to write. I recalled my mom entertaining herself on her Steinway & Sons in another room; the beauty of her music must have transported me because I didn't remember what I had written, I only remembered a stirring inside me, a natural high like a kite floating in the air, as I basked in the desire to create and express myself in words. This stirring was later acknowledged and affirmed, on separate occasions, when I won an elementary school writing contest and got published in a local newspaper. I should have known then that there was something inside me.

I should also have remembered another truth. In my middle school years, anger also clued me to the existence of my stirring. This time, it was through a monologue contest. Instead of acting out a few lines from a play or short poem, I had memorized an entire Dr. Seuss book and delivered it as if I had air under my feet and wings that stretched across the sky. I caught how the judges froze and fixed their eyes upon me as I let myself fly, and yet they disqualified me for exceeding their time requirements; I wanted to cry. And though my spirit's crushing converted to anger, it was clear the stirring was still there, living and breathing inside me, everywhere.

And I should have remembered yet another truth. In my high school years, at the brink of young adulthood, the written word and the spoken word came together, working in tandem. The stirring grew in constant fusion, as I won almost every oratorical contest I ever entered, was editor-in-chief of the *Columbia High*

School Capital Newspaper, wrote a short story that was published in a statewide student anthology, and was elected class speaker to deliver my high school graduation speech.

There, at MLK Chapel, standing, reminiscing on stage, and watching the graduates file in, I remembered those truths about myself as life came full circle. It was as if I had discovered myself for the first time, even though I had been manifesting all along and long before this very moment.

But somewhere in that circle, I was cursed by a long span of forgetfulness; the kind that resulted from distractions, the choice to give up most of myself to feel like I could belong, and the preference of pursuing a high-paying career over one I could build around my stirring. I yielded to a pressure, an expectation, whether self-imposed or not, to "be realistic" and find a job that would pay my bills, give me a good lifestyle, and thus satisfy the expectations of family. Meanwhile, the "real" Juliet, whose voice *was* her identity, the stirring that *was* her gift, which she first connected to at eight years old and developed as a teen, was gradually reduced into a remnant, only to be found in the dust of her dreams, waiting to be remembered and longing to be set free.

It was almost as if the universe directed every discomfort to center me and restore me back to purpose. Because in those moments of darkness or struggle, I was always gifted with a path forward, a path of least resistance; an outlet for me to take off the mask, find relief and validation, and share my value.

With Jed, I tapped my feet in a barren theatre and found joy performing to eight kids and a teacher. As a new consultant, the only Black and only woman at the table on my team who often felt excluded, I received validation and reward in leading the drama ministry at church and impacted a small congregation. After Zambia, I wrote and directed a community play on a respected stage and impacted the lives of many more people. With Kyle, I took a risk and moved to an unknown role to get closer to a version of a stage, and my visibility soared inside and outside the company as a result. With every way of escape, the "real" Juliet showed up while the stirring developed and refined itself along the way, preparing and leading me to the next big opportunity to serve a greater number of people—like now, where close to 1,500 people waited for me to take the podium.

Yes, it was in those happenstance moments, those periods of serving others, where the unexpected opportunities showed up the most and revealed to me my value and who I was supposed to be—not a business book, not a personality test, and not my education, title, or income. Even the opportunity to speak at this commencement ceremony might not have occurred if it weren't for my service on the South Fulton Chamber of Commerce Board of Directors alongside the campus president of this military college, who witnessed my special value and pursued it. My eyes widened with the realization of these undeniable truths.

And now, in front of all of these people, I took off my mask to reveal my authentic self as I stood in spotlight. I was ready to use that same voice to uplift the young hopefuls to "choose excellence"—my theme—in all they did so that they might live their best life.

Nothing could match this feeling of letting out the stirring because it was where the sun shined on me the brightest, where my uniqueness sang the loudest, and where people haloed me like a champion. All I knew was that I wanted to live in this stirring each and every day, regardless of whether it "fit in" into a traditional job description, because it was my honest gift, the fruit I produced to add value and light into the near and distant world around me.

It was time for me to deliver.

I stood at the podium against an austerity of high, thick golden organ pipes that loomed like pious elders in the distant backdrop. A warmth started rising from the nape of my neck as I felt the eyes of the military officers and school officials behind me. But I wasn't afraid. My confidence bore the weight of a mountain. I peered into a moving river of black caps and swinging tassels and took a deep breath. And, of course, I smiled. A calm suddenly washed over me as if I were home, and once I opened my mouth to speak, my voice hooked the audience like music as it breezed throughout the chapel.

"Excellence is a choice," I said as I got into the heart of my speech.

My words soon took flight as I highlighted the story of the company founder I admired, an ordinary man who did extraordinary things. I shared heartwarming stories of a few students—made them stand up and be recognized—who had triumphed over their own adversities. I encouraged the wisdom of choosing excellence in character, people, and work; words that would otherwise be hollow had I not faced oppositions of my own, the pressures that had quickened me in the darkness and aloneness, the fire as well as the flood.

There was a mixture of captivated silence, thoughtful reactions, a few cheers, and even tears throughout my speech. And then, I brought it all home.

"Because, Class of 2015, when you choose excellence, you will immediately begin to stand out and separate yourself from the pack. When you choose excellence, you will establish yourself as a leader that others will want to follow. Your value will increase and people will begin to notice you and respect you more. When you choose excellence, you begin to live life with purpose and intentionality, and every decision you make, from how you keep your house to how you dress and carry yourself to the financial choices you make are all elevated to a higher standard. When you choose excellence, you begin to recognize the people you need to keep in your life and the people you need to let go because you refuse to compromise who you are. When you choose excellence, you will develop a habit of making good, sound, and wise decisions for your life, decisions that bring blessings and that keep you out of harm's way.

"And finally, when you choose excellence, Class of 2015, companies will want to hire you, floodgates of opportunity will open up, people will give you preferential treatment, promotions will come, salary raises will be given, your name will be made great, and every other good thing will find *you*."

A sudden burst of applause erupted from the audience, long enough for me to swallow and catch my breath.

"Class of 2015, in closing, you don't have to compromise to be recognized."

"All right!" someone yelled out from the floor.

"With anything and everything you do, choose excellence... choose excellence...choose excellence. Congratulations! I salute you all."

The students, faculty, and guests all honored me with their shouts and generous applause as the beaming campus president met me at the podium to present me with a plaque.

It was as if the heavens opened up to me in that moment, enfolding me in the glorious rays of the spirits of the elders, Grandma Mattie and Grandma Ethel. My face warmed as I imagined them both stretching forth their hands to touch me. *Atta, girl...you did that!*

My career had finally met my call.

The "real" Juliet stood before the graduates, victoriously, as in a baptismal awakening, with her angled hand raised to her forehead in final salute. I was finally on a stage appropriate for me, being the company spokesperson and ambassador I had always longed to be, where I could share the company's story in a captivating, inspiring voice in the larger community.

This was perfection.

CHAPTER 8

Prepare for the Pivot

And yet, sadly, I could not escape *this* truth—not everybody rejoiced with me in my success. Not everybody saw, or even appreciated, the value in giving me work that embraced my gifts. Not everybody made agreements to further develop me in the work I excelled in the most. I learned, therefore, how effective my success was based on the level of those who opposed me.

After delivering my commencement speech, my feet sprang with the light step of happiness. But as I breezed about the office, I was stung by the quiet glares and pursed lips of a huddled few in the department. I imagined their hushed whispers fabled a disgracing of sorts upon me.

Hence, it didn't bother me that there were no balloons hanging in my office. No cards or handwritten notes of congratulations scattered my desk. No "way to go!" voicemails or impromptu recognitions at team meetings surprised me for achieving this honor. Even the glowing email from a military college officer to the company, which I was copied on, received an anemic response. I stopped expecting any form of validation which *was* my norm, once, under the thoughtful and supportive leadership of Josh and T.J.; I didn't work on their teams anymore. Different leaders created different cultures, and in lieu of any encouragement on *this* team, I was offered rebuke—for not seeking permission or approval to accept the honor of being a commencement speaker.

I had neglected to kiss the ring.

It was true; I had made many mistakes throughout my corporate career. I asked for forgiveness more than I asked for permission, something taught to me by the White male leaders who governed the company. Whether or not they intended that message for me, I still found the advice to be quite useful in my leadership ambitions.

This led to a transgression I could not escape, a tension that grew between me and my leaders with every win as of late: the visibility of working directly with the executive office; the serendipitous connections with elected officials, community leaders, and corporate executives; the appearance on the cover of a community magazine with a vice president of the company; the media interviews to promote the work I did in storytelling and external relations; and of course, the commencement speech and subsequent growing number of speaking requests. I championed myself first and didn't wait on a "sponsor" who might never have come. Thus, my *persistence* to grow and lead in the area of my strength created a noise for those who wished to silence me.

With every test and triumph, the "real" Juliet was emerging. Now, there was a steadiness in my eyes, a lift in my chin, a fire in my belly, and a straightness in my posture that altogether reflected my internal resolve. It was in my work, in my stirring, where I presented the truest and most honest version of myself, and I sprayed this self-assuredness like perfume that wisped in the air. It ruffled the feathers of those who obliged themselves to determine the limits of my success.

That was an agreement I refused to make any longer, regardless of my six-figure salary and company badge. It was painful enough, now, for me to realize that money was never worth the misery of self-denial. I couldn't continue living life in a cage, no matter how fancy it was, shackled by everyone else's expectations of me. And by age forty, with my own sanity at stake, I found myself at such a crossroads where I had to finally own my power and choose what was best for me.

Either way, the writing was on the wall.

"What do you want?"

That was one of the most important questions in the world, probably up there with *Will you marry me?* And the only thing more important than the question was the answer.

As I sat at a lunch booth in my company's café with Denise, who asked the question, my face got long.

"I'm looking at you. I can see you're not happy." Her raspy voice cut through my thoughts as her hands stretched open in my direction. "What do *you* want?"

I averted my eyes and cleared my throat, while smoothing my skirt with sweaty palms. I wasn't ready for this interrogation.

Denise was like a shot of caffeine, not much for small talk, packed with a lot of punch, and always on the go-go-go with her entrepreneurial ventures. An aspiring media mogul, she published an Atlanta community magazine, and it was on the cover of one of her spring editions where I was pictured with one of the company leaders to help promote the customer tours I led. I was given a goal to double the tour traffic and was working hard to achieve it. Apparently, some people in the company didn't like that my face was on the cover with this company leader, even though *he* had summoned me to join him in the picture.

I took a deep breath and broke my silence. "I want to speak. I *love* to speak. I love a stage, actually, but for the purpose of inspiring people. I've told you all this before. I wish I could travel all over the country, sharing the company's story, a message of leadership...be its spokesperson in that way." And then, my voice took on a low, meek tone. "I see myself writing books, too."

Denise nodded, while examining my face. "So, what's holding you back?"

I shrugged. "My leadership only wants me to focus on tours now. They don't want me out, they want me in...inside this building."

"But that's not what *you* want, is it?"

I looked down, shaking my head, too embarrassed to tell her how my glorious corporate career was all a façade. I was miserable. The office environment I walked into became so thick with tension I felt like I couldn't breathe. I was no longer included in my department's leadership meetings, and now I had to get approval for any opportunity to speak, whether it was for the company or even on my personal time at a weekend church service. In my earlier career under the leadership of Josh and T.J., those opportunities would have been encouraged.

"So, Juliet, *why* are you still here?"

Her questions gave me an awkward chill, as if I were stripping myself naked in a doctor's examination room. My stomach roiled in knots thinking about the luxuries I would have to give up: the free medical benefits, free lunches, adventurous retreats at beautiful resorts, occasional travels in the corporate jet,

international leadership missions, numerous leadership development opportunities, and the respect and exposure of working
for an admired brand. There was access to so many resources I
didn't want to leave behind, and above all, my income had grossed
into the top percent of the country. I rested in the comforts, privileges, safety, and predictability of working for this company. I
didn't know how to create this structure for myself if I left.

But at my core, and with all of those amenities, I still had not
reached a sense of personal fulfillment—that I was maximizing
the best of my human potential. I only had that when I stood
behind the podium to give that commencement speech. Just the
thought of it was like a hug to the universe, a testament to my
soul that I was alive, indelible, and relevant. Exercising my gifts
was my oxygen and my power—a sort of power that seemingly
my leaders didn't want me to have. Instead of being celebrated,
I was criticized and confined inside a company that shut this
power down. My heart neared a flatline from the containment
and boredom.

"I just haven't figured it out yet," I admitted, "but I don't think
I'll be here for much longer."

I paused to glance at Denise, who was only a year older than
I. She stopped eating her salad to study me. I stilled my hands,
which were twiddling a straw wrapper on the table.

"You know," I continued, "I started working here when I
was in my mid-twenties. On my first day, before I even walked
into the building, I just knew I wouldn't be here forever, that I
wouldn't retire here. I just couldn't see myself growing old in this
company. You know how you feel things but can't explain them?
It's almost like a prophecy." I lifted my face, searching the air for
my next thoughts, and softly chuckled with a mist in my eyes.
"I told myself I would only leave this company for one of three

reasons. I'd get married and work from home, go to Hollywood, or write a book. Those were the only three reasons I would leave this company—*not* to work for another corporation. Ten years...I gave myself ten years of working here when I started. I hadn't planned on being here this long. Almost sixteen years..."

"There's nothing holding you back, Juliet, except you. This company might not be where you're supposed to be. It was good for you at one point. But now? It may be time. And look at how much you've grown since you've worked here. Maybe this company was meant to prepare you for whatever is next. But listen, you'll be good for nothing if you're not happy."

Water welled in the corner of my eyes.

"You want to be a speaker, Juliet? A spokesperson? Yeah, I totally see it. You could be on television. You have so much presence. I watched you light up on stage when you spoke at that graduation. You have to *show* people that. People need to see the work you're doing. Are you on social media?"

"Girl, no!" I winced, leaning back into the booth. I put my hand up and shook my head. "I'm not into that. It's a waste of time. I see how addicted people are to it—I'd rather be reading a book. And I don't like putting my business out like that. I'm too private."

"No, Juliet! You need to use social media the right way. Show where you are, the work you do. Use it to show people in the light you want to be known for. If people don't *see* you as a speaker, how else would they know you like to speak?"

Denise had a point, even though the thought of being on social media unsteadied me. I was not an early adaptor to anything, and social media struck me as self-promoting in an unauthentic and vain way. I preferred the more tried and true method of promoting: word of-mouth. It seemed to be working for me so far, much to the chagrin of a few people on my team.

"I'm on Facebook, but that's it. I rarely post anything, just occasionally read other people's posts."

"Tonight—I want you to open a Twitter and Instagram account. *Tonight*. Then, follow me on my social media channels so that I know you're there, and I will follow you back."

"But I don't know how."

"Girl, pssh!" She swatted the air as if my comment were a fly. "It's easy. Just create a login. And post something...anything. Something fun. Nothing heavy. Post a picture, a video of some event you've attended. You attend events all the time!"

My eyes drooped with a measure of uncertainty, perhaps even fear. I didn't know whether to be silent and still or to be bold and courageous. I had never thought of social media as a stage, as a vehicle to build my cyber presence with positive messaging, but it *was* a path forward that my adversaries couldn't control or dictate, a small breath of freedom that couldn't be usurped. And yet, I suffered from a gnawing sense that creating a new buzz, when I knew my leaders wanted me to be quiet and focus *all* my energy on the work they assigned me, would backfire.

And so, *this* war ensued inside me: either behave and conform to what the company wanted me to be, or break free from the control they had over me. A lot was at stake.

Under the table, I balled my fists, digging my nails into my palms, hoping it would dull the drumming inside my chest. I knew the risk of my choices, that either would result in something lost and something saved. There was no middle ground.

"I know it feels uncomfortable now," Denise said, "but the more you do it, the easier it gets." My eyes met hers as she put the final stamp on our conversation, as if she had already witnessed my imminent end. "Get yourself in position, girl. *Now.*"

It all started with office space and business cards, though really, my presence was never really welcomed there in the first place.

After completing a successful year-long thirteen-city tour to launch the company's new mission statement, I finally moved into a public-facing role that allowed me to represent the company and tell its story. I was ecstatic.

After yet another company restructure, my role was assigned to a different team under the leadership of Connor Rumpkin, or Con, who had been around the company, and in the same role, for years.

I was chosen to help lead and work alongside a very green and young team. But not long after my arrival, I immediately sensed an "X" on my back, a hesitancy to accept me, perhaps in fear of the unknown. The employees knew I carried weight from working many years as a consultant, one of the most influential roles in the building. And since there weren't many Black women in leadership positions at all in the company—none were in the C-suite nor even on a VP level—they probably didn't know what to make of me, a well-put together woman who was known for being direct.

I asked to move into a vacant office with a window instead of taking a smaller aisle office where the young team members sat. It seemed reasonable, as I was in a senior leadership role. But then, I detected a sourness in the air, a sense of displeasure. I caught the faint hellos and cutting eyes as I walked into my office many mornings.

And then there were the business cards. Mine were a bit more expensive than theirs. That became an issue, too. I caught a whiff of the rumblings, "Why does *she* get to be different?"

Con, my boss, told me so.

It didn't matter that his business cards were the same as mine, or that he had an office with a view. They recognized him as the only leader on the team and were devoted to him.

I understood their feelings. I also remembered my uneasiness, at first, when T.J. became my leader. I had filled my head with all of these notions, thoughts like what kind of leader he would be and whether he would be kind and supportive like Josh, my first leader, whom I adored and who gave me unlimited access to him. There was safety in having access, that safety of an open door to confide in someone you know and trust. I went through the same feelings again when Kyle became my leader.

Like Josh, Con was many of these employees' first leader. With my coming onto the team to help Con lead it, perhaps they thought I threatened that access.

I did what I could to build relationships, to ease the tensions. I attended a church service with one, extended lunch invitations to others, or just sat in their office chatting and sharing stories. But I couldn't do it alone. I needed Con to support my leadership on the team, too.

Con was effective at crossing wires, I thought, instructing me with an area of responsibility but then giving the same—or even a different—responsibility to someone else on the team without communicating it to me. It brought about the sort of frustration, lack of role clarity, and confusion that, over time, bled the strength out of me. This was a different culture than the structured one I was used to in my previous role as a consultant, where I worked with older and more seasoned business people.

"You do really good work, Juliet," Con had told me in his office one day after an unpleasant exchange between me and one of the young team members. A junior employee had stepped into my office to give *me* a work assignment, as if I reported to her, and Con condoned it. "This is a small team, and very familial," he continued, "and you have to work on your relationships. We all share the work on this team, and they feel like you're condescending to them, that you *lord* over them."

I hadn't given them any assignments, never directed or mandated anything to them. In fact, after several weeks of transitioning into this new role, Con *still* hadn't figured out who would be reporting to me.

"What have I done to make them feel that way? Can you give me examples?"

"You always mention that you were a consultant before you moved to our team."

"Part of the reason I am even on this team is because of the relationships I have from my previous work as a consultant. Why is *that* a problem?"

"Well, you just don't have to bring it up all the time."

As my eyes shifted around Con's office, I noticed a few faded certificates and dust-coated plaques that clung to the walls. A picture of him and a senior company officer holding golf clubs was propped on a table behind him. Given his tenure and relationships with the company, I couldn't understand why my work history was an issue.

"You brought me on this team to help lead it. Why won't you support me?" My eyes pleaded.

"I *do* support you."

"But it's like you're so quick to take their side. These team members need to hear from you—and be clear—about my role on this team. I understand you all have close relationships. But it's challenging—and feels disjointed—when you give them work without running it through me first, and then you want me to follow behind them."

"I don't have to run anything through you. If I want to give them an assignment, I can."

I paused, shut my eyes and took a deep breath, trying not to let my frustrations escalate through my voice. There I was, brought on this small team to help lead and build it, but instead, I felt undermined.

"You know, Con, people outside this team talk."

"I don't care what people say," he shrugged.

"Well, they use words like 'dysfunctional' when describing this team." I paused, wondering whether I should keep going. I had been with the company long enough to see examples of great leadership, and the fool in me cared enough to not want him nor our team to be mocked. And so it happened, as it always did with me; I opened my mouth. "And, I, well, I don't think your leadership is consistent with the standard displayed by others in your position."

There. I said it. I thought by being honest and transparent he would see that I was sincere, that I was on his side. But I *was* a fool in that moment because no one really likes truth-tellers.

Con's wrinkly face turned hard as stone while a mist formed on his forehead. The two peering gray holes in his face almost swallowed me. There was no heartbeat behind those eyes, just emptiness, as if he had nothing to cherish in his life except the status the company gave him.

He leaned forward in his chair. "Look, if you don't like the way I lead, then you can leave this team!"

It was as if he punched the air out of my stomach. The same person who had just said I needed to work on my relationships seemingly didn't care about the relationship he had with me.

Our relationship was never the same after I stormed out of his office, and for the months that followed, the public-facing work that gave me so much strength was slowly stripped from me, especially as my number of speaker requests grew after my commencement speech. As time went on and the team expanded, I was pushed down the leadership hierarchy and restricted from any more external involvement, professionally or otherwise. I was reminded that jobs changed all the time, and Georgia was an at-will state.

Keep your head down...don't say anything...don't rock the boat... just be grateful you still have a job that pays well with good medical insurance. Those voices, those old souls from an ancient generation, swirled in my head to temper me. But I couldn't be "fixed." All the money, comforts, and privileges the company provided could not fill the black hole growing inside of me.

And there was more, much more over time, to this descent into corporate hell. There were frequent meetings with human resources. I felt isolated from my team. The senior vice president who once favored me and was my biggest cheerleader and praised my leadership capacity reneged on all his previous affirmations of me. "I'm losing confidence in your ability to lead. You've struggled with relationships for a while." He added, as an afterthought, "But, I like your *smile.*"

Frustration boiled in my body until the mental straps that held me together stretched and popped, and I found myself coming apart at the seams. That old familiar Goliath had resurrected and imposed itself like a wall, putting *all* the blame on me.

Every day was a fight. The distant sound of Con's voice in the hallway raised the hairs on my arms and made my heart palpitate. I woke up in paranoia, not knowing what value my life had in the company anymore, and I fell asleep at night with needles poking in my head.

I sought counseling to help me process and recover some clarity, and it all came down to this—I was too empowered and couldn't contain myself within the box I was assigned. My presence was strong. My self-assuredness was strong. My opinions were strong. My voice was the best and the worst of me, a Black woman in corporate America. And for the days that remained for me in *this* company, I hung around like a Gen X fossil, hollow, doing desk work—all because I had stood up to my leader.

"I've got forty-five months to make some things happen!"

That's what I told my friend, Jerome, who chuckled and shook his head while taking another bite of his sea bass. We were having lunch at The Optimist, a high-end hotspot in the posh, foodie-frenzy Westside district of Atlanta. The ambience in the restaurant always flared with some of the "who's who" in the city. It was our 2016 new year's brunch and a long overdue meeting we had scheduled in the middle of January.

"Why forty-five months?" Jerome asked.

"I'm trying to hang in there to make twenty years with the company. I don't know if I'll make it, though." I sighed, looking around the restaurant. "There's a 'more' to my life. I just don't know what it is yet. My expectations the past year have been... unmet."

Jerome cleared his throat, as if trying not to laugh, while still chewing on his food. The corners of his eyes lifted with amusement.

"You know, some people are quietly watching you, Juliet. People in the community, looking at you like the next person to watch out for. You have a presence. It's like, I could see you representing me in a boardroom in my absence. I know you'd always say the right thing."

Jerome's words soothed my spirit, but it wasn't enough to stop the taunting whispers in my head. A transition out of the company was imminent for me. I just didn't know when.

And worse, I didn't have a plan.

"What do you want to do?" Jerome asked.

I hesitated at the question, once again, feeling like my dream was fluffy, vain, and unrealistic, or perhaps just foolish.

"I want to be a spokesperson...*the* spokesperson...for the company, but it doesn't look like that's going to happen for me." I played around with the steamed veggies on my plate. There was nothing inside me to feed. "And I don't want to move to another department in the company to do work that doesn't fit me. I want to be able to speak and inspire people. That's what makes me feel strong."

Jerome looked at me with a tenderness that let me know he understood. He was an award-winning media marketing executive who embodied the smooth, old-school swag of Billy Dee Williams but with the charming youthfulness of the late Chadwick Boseman. Always dressed in a sports jacket, he strutted wherever he went, distinguished by his manicured goatee dusted with specs of gray. "You have value, Juliet. Most people give me their business cards, thinking their value is what comes after their names, after the comma. Nope! Your value is what comes *before* the comma."

Jerome's wisdom was a fresh breeze. I nodded. My value *was* inside me, not in a title or a company, which could go at any time. My *gift* was my value, something I brought to the company and which the company could never take away.

"And no matter how hard it may seem for you now, it's not cancer!"

My neck instantly snapped at the C-word. I tilted my head and furrowed my eyebrows.

"I had cancer once," Jerome continued in between forks of his food. "If you can beat cancer, you can beat anything. That's how I approach life now. Whatever it is, no matter how bad it is, my response to it is, 'It's not cancer.'"

We both chuckled at his serious humor.

"What you need is a plan." He raised his cloth napkin to wipe his mouth and drank a bit of water. "What are you doing to promote yourself now?"

"Well, for now, I just post event photos on social media, so people see what I'm up to."

"You need more than pictures. What you need is a roadmap. Someone who can help you devise a strategy. You need a publicist. And I have the right person for you."

September is your last month with the company.

I lay in bed staring blankly at the ceiling when my heart began to pick up speed. I didn't actually hear the voice, but it rang loud in my thoughts and the words echoed inside my head. I stood up with a quick dose of adrenaline plunging through my veins as I was struck with unmistakable clarity.

Set up your business. Build your team. Sell your rental property. Save cash for your business. Agree to leave.

And that was that. It was as if I were Noah receiving instructions on how to build the ark. Everything was specific, simple and short, and above all, clear. I wrote everything down and froze. I didn't get moments of clarity like this every day, and it came to me fast like lightning. I was gifted with an exit plan.

Like an obedient servant, I went to work. It seemed a lot to accomplish in seven months, as it was already February, but if these instructions came from heaven—and I believe they did— then I knew it was possible.

The next day, I called my realtor, Thomas, and put my rental property on the market. The tenant who occupied my property was a good one. She kept the house clean, paid her rent on time, and never made noise.

"Let's notify the tenant first and give her first right of refusal," Thomas said.

"Okay, but I want top dollar for my house and she has to accept the house as-is."

The tenant got pre-approved for a loan within a week, and within three weeks, the house closed. I shook my head in disbelief at how fast it happened. I had been trying to sell my house for the past twelve years, and it finally sold at my asking price.

At the closing table, I met the tenant, a *sistah*, who couldn't have been more than thirty-two years old, dressed very professionally in a light-blue suit and scarf that hugged her neck. My heart melted as I sat across from her. She looked down most of the time, glancing every now and then at me while I skimmed through the papers. She didn't move, and she kept her hands clasped together on her lap, holding her breath, until I signed all of my closing documents.

"Is this your first house?" I asked.

"Yes, ma'am," was all she said with a quiet, sheepish smile.

"You know, this house I'm selling you, it was my first house, too. You've been a really good tenant. You took great care of my house. I'm glad to be selling it to you."

A lump formed in my throat as I realized I was parting with something valuable. I glanced across the table and saw moisture in her eyes, too; I recognized that look. It was the humbled look of triumph of realizing a long-awaited dream. On a whim, I took my checkbook out of my purse and wrote out a check, then reached across the table to hand it to her.

"For you, your first housewarming gift as a homeowner...for being such a great tenant."

It was a check for five hundred dollars.

The closing attorney's mouth dropped. Thomas looked around as if he didn't know where he was. And with tears welling in my eyes, I got up to give my tenant—now, a new homeowner—a hug.

There wasn't a dry eye in the room.

"Okay, just so you know," coughed Thomas, "this is *not* normal. This does not happen at the closing table!"

"No!" the closing attorney declared in agreement.

"Can we take a picture?" the new homeowner almost whispered, wiping her face. Her lips parted into the biggest smile as she looked at me, and I swelled with joy.

After our picture, I said my goodbyes and headed straight to the bank.

Check. The selling of my rental property was crossed-out from my plan.

About a week after selling my rental property, I received a letter in the mail from my 401(k) administrator with some good news. I had exceeded the saving limits of my plan and received a substantial check for the overage. With the money I had already stashed in savings, the sale of the rental property, and now this unexpected money from my 401(k) administrator, I now had six figures saved to start a business account.

Check. This was further confirmation that the epiphany I had was real. Things were falling into place like clockwork. I was in alignment and on track with the plan.

In late March, I called Dexter, my long-time CPA and a good friend, with news of my pre-imminent departure from the company.

"What?" was all he could say. I heard his pen drop through the phone.

"I don't know when, Dexter." Actually, I did, but it didn't need to be discussed at that moment. "I just want to be in position for when it happens. What do I need to do to set up a business?"

I met with him the following week at his office. We discussed the type of business I envisioned. Then he drew the paperwork for me to get set up as an S-Corp.

"What do you want to name your business?" he asked.

I paused, not really giving it any thought. That wasn't a part of my Noah's Ark instructions. "Let's just name it after me for now."

A few weeks later, Dexter called me back into his office. My S-Corp binder, complete with an official letter from the Secretary of State, EIN, and shares of my business, were now officially part of my property.

"Congratulations," he said, handing me my binder. "Go ahead and start your business account. You mentioned you saved some seed money, right? Transfer that money over and save all of your business receipts."

I nodded.

Dexter shook his head in disbelief. "You are one blessed woman."

I took a deep breath and pinched myself. Everything so far was moving according to plan.

"You're going to need a board for your company. Have board meetings at least once a year. You're the president of your company. Who do you want on your board?"

"I don't know." My eyes wandered around the office before landing back on Dexter. "Well, what about you? Will you be my treasurer, since you're already my CPA?"

"Okay, that's not a problem. I serve in that role for some of my other business clients."

"And here's the name of my business attorney," I added, as I handed Dexter her card. I was good friends with this attorney, someone who played tennis with me often. I knew she would support me. "She can be my legal counsel. There. I have you to handle my taxes, and her to keep me from getting sued! That's a good team, right?" I chuckled at myself, knowing the two of them would make a sound board for me. I felt completely safe with them; they were good at what they did, they had both known me for years, and most importantly, they believed in me.

I just started a business, debt-free. After leaving Dexter's office, I treated myself to a ribeye steak and a glass of wine. I reflected on how people saved for college, a house, a vacation, or their children's education. But I wondered, how often do people save for a business?

Check. My business was official.

But I wasn't done with my list just yet. While I had a board, I still needed people around me to help develop my vision.

I eventually met and began working with the marketing professional Jerome suggested. Her name was Carly, and I liked her immediately. While I was restricted from speaking anywhere or conducting media interviews, I did let her build up my social media presence, and together, we brainstormed ideas for building a future personal brand. Her encouragement was priceless.

"Everything you're going through, everything at that company, has an expiration date. It won't last forever." Carly's words were like balm, and she always made me feel as though I was her only client.

Within the first month of working with her, she scheduled a weekend photo shoot with one of Atlanta's best artistic photographers whose work was often seen in magazines. The last shoot I had done was two decades ago, when I worked at the bank. Just the thought of having another opportunity for fresh photos rekindled an old, familiar vigor I once had when I thought I might go to Hollywood.

Check. This was the beginning of my team: a CPA, a business attorney, and a marketing specialist. In addition to those three, I also had tight relationships with the presidents and CEOs of civic and non-profit organizations whose boards I served on, and they desired, to my delight, for me to remain on their boards pending my transition. And finally, I surrounded myself with business owners, like Denise, who all worked in corporate America before making their pivot into entrepreneurship. I leaned on all of their advice and encouragement.

Meanwhile, it was time for my annual performance review at the office. I had no expectations for a glowing report. I was given a stretch goal to double the tour traffic from the previous year. I and others worked furiously to reach this big goal but landed at 83 percent or so of obtaining it, which wasn't too shabby.

However, the performance review given to me now was unlike any other; it was so scathing and skewed it was novel.

She plays the victim...she's not a team player...she doesn't accept responsibility...she struggles with peer relationships...she doesn't meet any of the core values of the company....

And it went on and on. Every category of the performance review was unsatisfactory, except one, my "Drive for Results" which received a satisfactory score. I had never received a performance report like that in all my years in corporate America. Overall, I always met expectations.

I sat in the chair, numb and nonreactive, because I knew those words did not define me.

But that night, and for so many nights thereafter, memories of all I had done for the company played like a slow song in my head; the celebrations of helping clients I consulted write their first profit check, the benchmarking trips I took my teams on, the young aspiring leaders I mentored, the countless encouragement and prayers, the coworkers' children I supported, the marriages and baby showers and funerals I attended, the people around the world I touched in a room or from a stage, and every other memory from all those years that was carved into my life and could never be erased.

My face flushed and streaked with tears as if it had been slapped a thousand times. I clutched myself in my prayer closet, lamenting that the company I loved didn't love me back. And while there were at least two sides to every story, including mine, I bowed my head in submission to this *final* truth: I had outgrown this company culture, and it was time for me to go.

"God," I prayed, "please give me courage. Get me out of this valley! And if the company doesn't want me as its spokesperson, then please elevate me and make me yours."

Amen.

A few months later, in late June, I received a phone call from a representative in human resources.

"Heath would like to meet with you. Are you available to meet with him this week?" The call was unexpected, odd even. I didn't have much interaction with Heath, a senior manager in human resources.

"How should I prepare for the meeting?" I asked.

"There's nothing you need to do to prepare. He just wants to talk to you." Her voice was so light and squeaky, like a little mouse. People in human resources have a gift of mastering ambiguity. It was annoying.

"Well then, what's the meeting about?" *Just spill the beans*, was what I really wanted to say.

There was a pregnant silence at first. I gripped my phone tightly, tapping my left foot, waiting for a response from this timid woman on the other line.

"To be on the same page."

And with those succinct, measured words, my mouth dropped and I sat down. And while it wasn't quite September yet, I knew the time had finally come for me to check the last box.

CHAPTER 9

Grieve, Then Grow

"Hey, Juliet! Great to see you again. Come on back."

I stood up immediately. Dr. Sue, my therapist, always greeted me with a smile as wide and sincere as mine. I first began seeing her several months before I left the company and appreciated how she met me with herself at the reception area. She was always so personable that way.

"Thanks for making time for me." My words wavered a bit as I shifted my eyes and looked down at the floor. My stomach churned.

Together, we walked down a short hallway and into her office, a space brushed with calm seaweed tones and subtle accent lighting that reminded me of a day on the beach. Like small ocean waves crashing, the room whispered, *It's okay. You can relax now. Breathe.*

I grabbed a throw blanket and plopped onto an oversized suede chair that swallowed me. It had been several weeks since my final departure from the company and corporate America altogether. Since then, little birds had told me how some

people thought I was crazy for leaving. And there was specula-
tion around my departure, why I had gone. Most relationships
from the company I had intentionally left behind; it was simply
better that way. I didn't need their opinions and nosiness to add
to my increasing anxiety.

"So, how is it going?" Dr. Sue grabbed my attention and fixed
her eyes upon me with interest. Her ruffled bangs gave her a
somewhat relaxed and youthful disposition, even though I
guessed she was in her late fifties. She eased back into her chair
and crossed her legs. A pen and notepad rested on a small table
beside her, though she seldom wrote anything down during
our time together. She took a sip from her coffee cup, awaiting
my reply.

"I have highs and lows," I said, staring at a corner in the ceiling. "I still have dreams...or nightmares. I was so loyal, you know.
It just hurts...still doesn't feel right." It was difficult for me to rec-
oncile that after all my years of service to the company, I could be
so expendable.

I dropped my eyes to the floor and squeezed the blanket,
attempting to stop the onset of tears. My emotions stretched in
every direction now. I was angry one minute, an uncontrollable
crybaby the next, then flat and numb, as if my entire body were
filled with Novocain.

"It's okay. I'm here to help you move on." Dr. Sue paused to let
her words settle. "Can I get you some water?"

I shook my head, then she continued.

"You're having these nightmares because everything—your
experiences and feelings regarding the company—still swirls in
the back of your mind. Your subconscious, it's working things
out." Dr. Sue's clear, focused eyes were wide with compassion,
her voice calm as a quiet stream. "You're grieving, Juliet, and it's

natural. It's a process, and anger is a part of that. People bounce back and forth through different stages, until you reach a place of acceptance. Even then, there may be times you feel emotional all over again. Grief happens whenever you lose, or you part with someone or *something* that's valuable to you...even the loss of a dream."

I took a deep breath and nodded. It had hurt to have a door shut in my face, to be rejected. It felt like something had been ripped inside me.

There weren't many people I could talk to who would understand why I *had* to leave, except my team—my CPA, attorney, and marketing consultant. They worked for companies once and decided they could do better working for themselves. But discussing grief required patience, something most people didn't have. I didn't even tell my own parents right away that I had left the company. They grew up at a time when Black people didn't have tons of access and opportunity, so they would never understand why I'd left behind so much security to jump into something ambiguous as being an inspirational speaker.

"What did the company mean to you?" Dr. Sue leaned forward. "Think about the years you spent there. In one word, what did it represent?"

It was more than a paycheck. More than medical insurance and six weeks of paid vacation every year that I could roll over. Despite some of my early struggles with exclusion and bias, I became attached to the company. It was where I lived life; where my birthdays were celebrated, where I cried with others who experienced loss, where going to my coworker's kid's soccer game was as natural and sincere as their kids calling me "Auntie."

"Family." I barely uttered the word under my breath, looking down. Water puddled in my eyes now. "It was like a family to me." I never married nor had any children, though I wanted them. Dating was especially difficult, since I traveled for much of my career. My mom, dad, and sister all lived in different states. And though I had a few friends, many of them were married. My church offered some support, although my attendance dropped after I went to grad school. But the company had been my anchor, my only constant for seventeen years. As an adult, it was the only major support system I knew.

Dr. Sue raised her eyebrows. "Say more."

"Well, I was young, still in the baby cart so to speak, when I started working for the company." I lifted my head to look at her before continuing. "It was like I was planted there. I guess, in some ways, I felt like I was raised there, where I developed the most professionally. I felt safe, protected...even accepted. Well, initially, I did, anyway. My very first group leader, Josh, was like a father figure, very kind and nurturing. He liked my spunk, my energy, I think. I met and got to know his family. He opened his home to me and other coworkers on the team. He was big on team bonding."

I paused, smiling. Josh was one of few people at the company who'd believed in my potential. "You've got raw talent, Juliet," Josh first said to me when he had offered me a job. I reflected on how good it felt to be seen, to just be given an opportunity.

"Go on," Dr. Sue gently prodded.

"Josh was my group leader for years before the organization restructured. He was always encouraging, always available, always gave me feedback to build me up in my career. I guess you could say *he* was the company to me."

"Hmm, I see. And company cultures change, especially when there is a change in leadership."

"Yep!" I nodded vigorously. Once the company founder died and changed CEOs, for example, loyalty became an old-school term.

"But you mentioned family, Juliet. That the company was like family...at least initially. Why don't you tell me about *your* family?"

"*My* family?" I was caught off guard.

Dr. Sue nodded. Her eyes warmed the room even though they had the ability to cut through a maze, to search for unspoken truths.

My shoulders tensed as I resurrected memories of my past. "Okay, well, I'm from Columbia, SC," I began, thinking of my hometown that boasted a confederate flag in front of its capitol. "All of my family is from there, though many of us live in different states now. I have an older sister, Annette. She's a doctor."

Dr. Sue smiled. "And your parents?"

"My mom was a music teacher and my dad fixed gas pumps. But they were both musicians and had a dance band...well, for a while. The band broke up, and well, later, so did they."

"Did they remarry?"

"Yes, eventually. My mom was first, though. The man she married moved in with us, in *our* house, and..." I turned my head towards the wall. "He was very controlling."

The air got thick anytime I thought of him, my stepfather, my mom's second husband. There were no candles in his eyes. I suffered the memory of how he moved about the house like a walking shadow, always brooding, while his footsteps pounded the hardwood floors. My heart raced.

Dr. Sue didn't move. I felt the rays from her stare penetrate into my consciousness. "So, what was that like?"

"Well, I, uh...I guess I don't have many fond memories." I decided to spare her the details of how anger poured over him like hot lava. When the world seemingly slammed every door in his face—he couldn't get a job, or rather, *keep* one—he filled his emptiness and need for respect with his dictatorship over women in the home. I jumped out of my skin whenever he said my name; he always yelled it like one does *"Stop!"*

Once, when I was a high school sophomore, my mom showed my straight-A report card to my stepfather, who just glanced at it and muttered in a gruff tone, "That's what you're supposed to do." There was never a nod or a smile. He didn't even look at me in my moment of success. Head down, I slumped back to my room and taped my perfect report card inside my bedroom door like a poster, so that every day, I encouraged and motivated myself.

Even then, at fifteen years old, I learned to become my own champion.

Dr. Sue was still as I told her that story about my grades. She waited on me to continue.

"And I couldn't date boys, and very seldom did I go out with friends. I had to watch the news every day, was restricted from watching mostly everything else, except sports. I stayed in my room mostly, reading books for entertainment. That was mostly my escape. And writing." I took a deep breath, pondering. "You know, I was a great student, a leader in school, church. I won awards. Always followed the rules. But he was critical, *always* critical, especially of me. My mouth got me into trouble with him a lot. I let them know when I didn't like something. He was just mean and miserable and...well, his hands were heavy." My face warmed with the memory of many stings. "Once or twice, he threatened to cut me off from seeing my own grandparents if I talked."

I rubbed my chest at the memory of Grandma Mattie and Grandma Ethel—and my grandfather, too. They were my respite, my nurturers, and the best of my teenage years.

I paused to glance at Dr. Sue, whose simple nod encouraged me to continue.

"And he prided himself with knowing scriptures. He thought he was the *only* biblical authority. He used religious terror tactics to put fear in me. He warned me that I might die an early death if I dishonored him."

Dr. Sue tilted her head ever so slightly.

"Crazy, right? Quoting scriptures about children who honor their mother and father are promised to live a long life...taking it out of context." I shook my head. "I was just a child, a young teenager."

Dr. Sue cleared her throat before taking another sip of her coffee. "And your real father? Where was he?"

My eyes lifted and a hint of a smile formed on my lips.

"Well, he had his struggles, too, trying to find his own way in life. Was absent for most of mine, though, as a teenager, after the divorce. But he finally got back on his feet and later remarried. He lives in Chicago now. We talk every Friday." My dad bloomed late in life. His own father had died when he was young and still trying to learn how to lead and be a man in an American culture that historically and systemically marginalized Black people.

I anticipated the next words on Dr. Sue's lips. It was a common textbook question.

"Do you think your experiences with your stepfather, or even your father, have affected your relationships with men? Maybe even men you worked with at the company?"

Probably, I thought, as I looked away and sighed.

"Because how we are shaped, how we show up as adults—at work, as leaders—often goes back to home, you know...with mommy and daddy."

But it was deeper, much deeper, than mommy and daddy, who both simply did the best they could with what they knew and how they were conditioned—including my stepfather.

This was about *triggers*.

There were certain triggers that produced a "fight" in me. Dictator-like authority was one. Attacks on women and the attempts to mute and subdue them were another. I couldn't stand the double standards between men and women, especially at work—like being assertive, passionate, and direct, and how such qualities were praised in one sex and condemned in the other.

My problems were not with men in general. I loved my grandfather *and* dad, even though he wasn't perfect. I admired and respected Josh and T.J. and had good relationships with them and several other men I worked with in corporate America. *My* problem was with a system, culture, or individual mindset that devalued women, especially Black women like me.

Puddles grew in my brown eyes. Like anyone else, I needed to feel accepted, valued, and free; a Black woman who could simply maximize her human potential without being silenced, slighted, shamed, and shut down. I found a box of tissues nearby and grabbed a couple. My words came out like a whisper. "I feel like I'm *always* fighting, Dr. Sue. And I'm tired...*so* tired."

My face wrenched into the tissues. Silence cloaked the room.

"What's done is done," she began gently after I surfaced and met her eyes. "You can't change your past nor what happened at the company. I think you simply outgrew the culture there. Perhaps the last department wasn't big enough for both you and your former leader. And maybe, unfortunately, you were just easier to let go. But that's all in the past now. *You* will get through this. And the fact that you have put together your own team—a CPA, lawyer, marketing consultant who've all agreed to help you, work with you—that tells me that you *are* a team player."

My shoulders relaxed. I offered Dr. Sue a small smile.

"Over the next few weeks, I want you to reflect and write down lessons learned from your work experiences. What you're most grateful for, what shaped you the most, what you can carry over into your new chapter. Journal them. And let's meet again next month."

I nodded and hugged Dr. Sue, then scheduled a date for my next session. I walked toward my car feeling a pound lighter.

And in time, with more and more counseling, I managed to work through my grief. Thereafter, the nightmares began to fade.

My home office had been more like a storage room. Swaying cobwebs laced the corners, piles of folders stacked the floor, and dust settled everywhere. But I cleaned it out, organized it, and made it into a working space. Before me now was a blank brown board, which I would soon make into my first vision board.

A voice. A resilient spirit. An ability to captivate a generation of people around the world, especially women. These were the images that had flashed inside me for years. I surfed through magazines, digital images and memes, pulled out favorite scriptures, and thought about my "why." And it all culminated into this assignment, or mission: *Deploy my gifts into the world until there is nothing else left for me to give.*

Per Dr. Sue's homework, I took into account all of my invaluable experiences and lessons from corporate America, which over the course of twenty years, had constructed and prepared me for my new chapter. I understood servant leadership, learned from a successful business model, and witnessed how generosity and building relationships were a great way to market and grow a brand. Most importantly, I had work to help me identify, or *remember*, my gifts and to refine them. Going to Zambia and to other countries on leadership missions gave me global exposure and a stage to practice public speaking. With the income I had made, I was able to save seed money to start a business of my own so that I could live and work without financial pressure.

I needed corporate America. Every experience, even the unpleasant ones, developed, toughened, and shaped me into the evolved woman I had become. Jed, Jackson, Con—and on a side note, even my stepfather—were as necessary to my development as Josh and T.J. I accepted this truth, and thus, I was capable to forgive. Because just like the biblical story of Joseph, who forgave his own brothers after they had betrayed and hurt him, bad experiences—and the pain and anger that flowed from them—still had purpose and could be used for good.

This was my vision; to become a global ambassador of hope and possibility who inspired people, through *my* gifts, to become the best and truest versions of themselves. I wanted to champion people, especially women, to remember their gifts and own their opportunities just as I had owned mine. No matter the opposition, there was always a path forward.

I sat back and looked at the clutter of all the magazine clippings, graphics, and quotes that represented my dream: an influential voice on stage and in media, a respected author, a champion of women, and a philanthropist. I posted my vision board in my bedroom, just as I had my report card when I was fifteen, to remind myself each day of the woman I was and would soon come to be.

"Bless this dream and finish the work you started in me," I said, lifting my face toward the ceiling.

Amen.

Behind the scenes, Carly, my marketing agent, was landing me speaking opportunities. One was in Buffalo, NY, for a women's empowerment organization, and another was in Washington, DC, for women entrepreneurs. I was also booked to speak at a statewide tourism conference, then later facilitated two civic leadership trainings. There were media opportunities, too, to discuss my transition from corporate America to starting my own business.

All of this happened within weeks of my leaving the company, in the late summer and fall of 2016. By December, I had my website up and running and I started writing a blog.

In 2017, I said yes to every speaking opportunity, whether I was paid or not. It was my way of "sampling" my product, or planting seeds, to further increase trial and awareness of my presence on the speaker circuit. I used the photos and videos from those events to develop more marketing collateral. By the end of 2017, I had completed eighteen speaking engagements and was recognized by a local media publication as one of "Atlanta's Black Women of Excellence."

I was having fun. The testimonies and feedback were positive. There was always at least one person in the audience who either commented about me on social media or connected me to other speaking opportunities. I was still just getting started and laying the foundation. I had a long way to go to achieve the level of greatness I posted on my vision board.

There was no feeling like this, no greater joy in my life thus far than just being myself and living in the fullness of who I was meant to be, for all the world to see. It was the best kind of freedom.

Now I could believe what people commonly said, that when God closes one door, He opens another. What they left out was that, sometimes, the door He opened was actually a backdoor, like a secret passageway, that led to a dry and dark valley. It was necessary for me to walk the path of utter humility—to be tested, learn a lesson, gain experience, and build character—before I could shine in my fullness. And for that, I found God to be incredibly complex, and yet still a genius, because there was always the opportunity to be restored back to purpose, to get back on the path to destiny; even for me, a woman over forty. And thus, I concluded that there really were no mistakes in life, no failures that could destroy a person forever. There were just open doors and closed ones—a redirection of sorts—even though it was still up to me, and no one else, to decide whether to move through the open doors or remain stuck in the hallway.

And *that* was my truth.

CHAPTER 10

Keep Growing

Juliet,

I just wanted to take a minute to thank you personally for all of your wisdom, encouragement, and advice that you shared with us at Junior League. I attended the event not knowing what to expect and with no real expectations, just this desire to start getting serious about making my life what I want it to be. I left feeling so uplifted by your words, I know I was meant to be there that morning!

I think one of the most profound pieces of wisdom you shared was that unveiling our "purpose" or true gift should be easy! Instead of embarking on a lifelong journey to discover what our talents are, it's more about what feels natural and easy. Humans make things so much harder than they need to be sometimes by overthinking what we should leave to gut instinct. I do a pretty good job of trusting my gut in relationships and friendships but I never thought about applying that to my professional life, too!

I was very inspired by everything you shared with us and truly admire your grace, intelligence, candor, and most of all that you're a powerful, independent, successful, badass woman! Looking forward to finding a way to utilize my strengths!

Thanks again,

Jane

Juliet,

Meeting you at the Women of Empowerment Conference was the most inclusive leadership I have ever experienced in my life. I want to thank you for helping me realize my sense of belonging and finding peace within my self-discovery. When I heard you speak on that day, I was compelled to learn more from you. I have listened to your recorded talks, "Leadership in the 21st Century" and "When You Hit the Glass Ceiling, Open a Window." These tools have helped me understand my existence. You sharing your story about growing up in a non-inclusive household gave me the focus I needed to realize my own self-doubt, fears, and values.

My life story is filled with a lifetime of non-inclusive leaders, self-doubt, fear, and pain. I have tried not to let the external situations control my life, but as I look back, I'm sure that I was not so successful at that as much as I would have liked.

I am the second born of five children. My mother lived a very hard life after leaving my father when I was about three or four years old. My father was the only inclusive force in my life. To this day, I can still remember his encouragement, unconditional love, and peace. I remember how happy I was every Friday when he would pick me up on the weekends, and how all I wanted was to be with my dad. I lost him when I was six years old, and he was 28 years old. That was the day my world would change for the worst. My mother remarried, her second husband was a very abusive man, beating her so badly for so many years.

Juliet, you asked how you channel a life of pain into a life of promise? I now know the true answer is faith, self-discovery, and confidence. I realize that my entire life has been to help people, to remove non-inclusive people from my life, to hold on to my vision, to survive and thrive. As I sit here writing you this letter, I am truly grateful for your words of wisdom. I am confident that I have to be fruitful and utilize the most important gift that God has given me from a young child.

To date, I'm a financial advisor. As a 22-year resident of Broward County, I have made it my objective to offer all residents the education that will help best position them for medical and financial security regardless of their current health or economic situation. Members of this community have been empowered by experiencing the positive impact of the education I provide. To date, I have over 350 private clients.

I feel determined. Thanks to you and the memory of my father, I'm more empowered than ever.

—Rebekah

Juliet,

Thank you for coming to My Sister's House. This was very informative and inspirational. For me, you were a confirmation of what God has been speaking. I will step out on a calculated plan. Thank you for being brave enough to step out and into what you have been gifted. Thank you for speaking so lovingly to us.

Inspired,
Tameka

"Where is your book?" A robust woman in a red dress browsed my table with a perfectly polished acrylic fingernail. Her thick arched eyebrows bunched together in either confusion or disappointment as she looked at the audio recordings of my previous talks. "I don't see it."

I froze. My heart thumped from embarrassment.

There, on a beach resort in Fort Lauderdale, FL, I was at the 2018 Women of Empowerment Institute Conference. Television personalities, national journalists, actors, and other influencers headlined the list of speakers. More than four hundred women were in attendance, and I was one of the invited speakers. Just minutes before, I had stood on stage as an authority of empowerment. Now, I wanted to put my head in the sand.

"It's coming," I said with a forced, wide grin. It was the best I could say to save face.

"Oh, okay," she replied, reading the back cover of one of my CDs she had picked up. "Well...I enjoyed your talk. I'll take this!" She handed the CD to my assistant for purchase, then wormed her way through the masses of other women to the next table with her oversized purse and swag bag.

I stood there, frozen. All the joy and euphoria permeating inside me from being on stage was eclipsed in that very moment. Without a book, all of my previous successes as a speaker—the multiple travels to various conferences across major cities, including an international trip to Ottawa, Ontario—vanished like a puff of air. There, in Fort Lauderdale, I was included on a speaker list with giants, and yet that woman in red left me at my own conference table feeling as tentative as a grasshopper.

It had been two years since I drove off the lot of the last company I worked for in corporate America. Since then, each day was like morning dew—a fresh start to spread my wings. New photo shoots, presentation rehearsals, team meetings, scripts, and run-of-show reviews never got old. I loved the speaker life and the process of building my brand—and even more so, the impact I was having on people.

Now that I controlled my schedule, I struggled creating a consistent structure of how to manage my time effectively. I was busy, but I wasn't always productive. So, when the lady in red spoke to me at my table, she was like an angel that appeared out of nowhere and was visible only to me. Her question was indelible. *Where is your book?*

With all the fun and fluff I'd been having in my new life as a speaker, I had ignored my internal voice, the voice of my Creator, which rendered me the single most important instruction that could enlarge my footprint and multiply my career—*write*.

My heart sank.

A few weeks after the conference, it was time for my annual fall board meeting with Dexter, my CPA, and Rachel, my business attorney.

Rachel and I were chums and played tennis together. But today, she held my feet to the fire.

"What are you doing with your time? When you're not speaking?" Her eyes bore into mine as if I were on trial, while Dexter continued scanning through my accounting documents. I fidgeted in my seat as the room got stuffy.

Sleeping in. Playing tennis. Dating. Socializing with my girl-friends over lemon drop martinis. Enjoying my freedom. And everything else I couldn't do while I was confined within the walls of corporate America. Though, I dared not admit this truth.

But I had been working, too. I reported on all of my accomplishments in 2018, my speaking and local media engagements, and my civic engagements. I stayed active on a couple of boards to keep myself visible and connected to corporate executives.

"And guess what? My biggest personal accomplishment this year was paying off my mortgage," I offered, hoping they would be impressed. "I'm completely debt-free!"

Dexter favored me with a nod, smiling. Dressed in suspenders, he oozed the comfort of an encouraging grandfather. Financially, I was still solid. I had prepared my life for entrepreneurship and saved a lot of cash to live on for a few years while I built my speaking brand. Most of the revenue I generated was invested back into my business. But for Rachel, my Ivy League attorney and tennis pal, it was as if my achievement went over her head. She stuck to my most important goal on paper.

"Your season of rest is over, Juliet. Either finish the book, or set a different goal that is important to you." There was no wavering in the tenor of Rachel's voice. She did not flinch.

"Yes, got it. Thanks for the accountability," I said sheepishly. "It'll be my number one priority in 2019. It'll get done; I promise!"

"A book can open more doors for you," Dexter chimed in like a good cop, "but you're doing okay...for now."

I left the board meeting feeling like I had been put in time-out, though I was grateful I had a team that cared enough to push me. With freedom came much responsibility. For the months that followed, as I continued to build my speaking career, I picked up the drafts of my three written chapters and began to write again.

And while there were highs and lows in my journey—and I still had to give an account for my time and work to my board—there was nothing that matched the feeling of my gifts growing inside me. My work felt so natural, like it was an extension of me. The letters, fan mail, and other testimonials I received in return rewarded me more than money itself. I was respected and valued, confirmation that I was exactly where I was supposed to be. It was powerful, the ability to grow and self-maximize without limits—except for those I had imposed on myself.

There were redemptive moments, too. A few people from my former company reached out to either congratulate me on the work they saw I was doing or to ask me for development advice. One of the markets I had consulted in my early years even invited me to speak to them.

This was the result of my owning my opportunities, the *process* of maximizing the gift inside me, and being bold and courageous enough to share it with the world. I was in the early stages of living my dream and empowering audiences, especially women, who aspired to discover and develop their own unique value and become more than what their cultures, traditions, or institutions wanted them to be.

After all, why be a glorified, unfulfilled laborer in someone else's kingdom when you can create your own?

For me, there were no regrets.

Author's Notes

I t is quite simple—humankind was not created to be restrained, trapped, or controlled. *Every* experience—every success and failure, gain and loss, acceptance and rejection, triumph and defeat, open and closed door—can restore us back to purpose and bring us into the fullness of the man or woman we were created to be.

Self-maximization, tapping into our own human-being-ness—the inherent qualities and unique abilities that define who we are—to become the best version of ourselves, is the gift we give to ourselves and to humanity. Ultimately, it is through our excellence in becoming, in living out our intended creation at the highest call, that we honor our Creator.

Isn't it interesting that as children, we were encouraged to dream? We were inspired to be anything we wanted to be if we put our mind to it. Then, as we got older, we were admonished to "be realistic"—to get an education and a job, get married and have children, pay our bills and our taxes—and die. *Being realistic* is an affront to human creativity, passion, faith, and childlike wonder, however. *Being realistic* imposes doubt, keeps you at bay, and reduces you to think safe and small. *Being realistic* crushes dreams and robs the human spirit that craves to be boundless and godlike. *Being realistic* kills self-maximization.

Hear this: Everyone is born with a unique ability, a gift or talent, that illuminates the true individual and the value he or she offers to the world. Life gives us every chance, every opportunity, every lesson to discover ourselves and our natural abilities. Reflect on that, pay attention. Even rejection, though painful, is something to celebrate because it redirects us to the right path we were meant to follow anyway.

And so, I can look back over my experiences and be grateful. There is no such thing as a perfect company, church, community, or childhood, because there are no perfect people. Those environments exist to help us grow and mature—to fertilize, water, crush, and germinate the seed of greatness inside each of us—and to hold up the magic mirror that exposes our truest character, our highest nature, and our most divine essence as human beings. We need the balance of both the good and the bad experiences to self-maximize.

It is our responsibility to own our opportunities. The hope is in us to maximize who we are, to be the absolute best version of ourselves—the man and woman God had in mind when He created us—so we can leave a meaningful legacy in this world and go out empty.

Reflecting on over my twenty years working for companies and pursuing opportunities to help me grow and self-maximize, I discovered the following keys to owning my opportunities.

I hope these lessons work for you, as well.

Recognize When You've Outgrown a Situation

Know when it's time to go and find the courage to make your move. Unfortunately, many people are unwilling to take the risk of leaving a situation that no longer benefits them. They choose to survive in their jobs rather than thrive in their calling, remaining stuck in misery or discontent rather than chasing their dream or seeking a new challenge that results in more growth, success, and freedom.

Below are three clues—there are certainly others, but I find most experiences can roll up to one of the three below—that informed me I had outgrown my situation in corporate America.

- **Attitude check.** Do you find yourself in a constant state of anger or bitterness, or perhaps easily annoyed or underappreciated in your current environment? Are your human needs—e.g., purpose, significance, security, respect, and a sense of belonging—being met? Do you carry a sense of dread, and are these feelings causing you to disengage or become disgruntled? If you've made attempts toward reconciliation (i.e. account for and correct your own human error), and these feelings persist, then consider seeking a different environment that will further expand your mind, meet your human needs, and ultimately, bring fulfillment.

- **Vision check.** Do you have a clear picture of where you're going from the person who's leading you? Can you support your leader/team even if you have a different point of view? Conflicts in vision—and values—will always produce frustration, disengagement, and division. If you once were excited but now possess a deep-seated tension when it comes to rowing in the same direction with your supervisor, team, or relationships in general, then it may be time for you to make a transition and move on.

- **Growth check.** Do you feel stuck or limited in your role? Are you wilting from a constant state of boredom? Once you stop growing, you begin to start dying. And by "dying," I mean you eventually lose your enthusiasm and relevance. As humans, we need to feel successful and like we're moving from one level to the next. If you're not getting opportunities that challenge you, or if there is no more room for you to grow in your current environment, then consider pursuing new opportunities that will encourage your growth and development, increase your value, and fuel your sense of self-worth.

Start Somewhere

Everyone dreams. Our dreams give us insight into our purpose. Where does your mind drift while driving to work, sitting in front of your computer, or lying in the bed? Like coming attractions, our dreams give us a preview to our future. They muse and encourage us with whom we are to become.

But our dreams will never come to fruition if we never act on them. Even if you're unsure of your dreams or the direction your life should go, just take a step in a direction...any direction. If you take a step and fail, you will learn a valuable lesson of what worked and what didn't. Then you can reset your life and start again.

There are many doors in life. Most of them will slam in your face, and for good reason. The few doors that remain wide open to you are the ones meant for you. But the key is to start. Take a step. Trust the open doors and the closed ones until you discover the correct path for *your* life.

It's on you to put things in motion. Get the ball rolling and start the journey from wherever you are with intentional and actionable steps—and never stop. Believe that you deserve the life you see in your dreams and then simply work toward it, one step at a time.

When pursuing my dream, especially toward the end of my corporate career, here are examples of how I started:

- **Write down what you see or create a vision board.** Begin with getting your imagination out on paper. If you keep your dreams locked inside you, they will continuously nag and frustrate the hell out of you, like a rabid dog rattling a cage. Have you ever felt this way? Perhaps this explains why many people become restless, depressed, and angry, because they're not moving in the direction of their desired future. You become less frustrated when you move the location of your dreams out of your head and onto a physical place where you can see it every day like a guiding light.

- **Create a plan.** Think through initial actions—just simple baby steps—you need to take toward your dream and compose it into a plan. If you want to become an actor, take acting classes. If you dream of becoming a lawyer, then spend time with other lawyers or register for the LSAT. If you want to write a book, take the first step of attending a writer's conference and learn from people who have published books. Ask yourself, "What is one thing I can do each day to position myself toward my dream?" Write your ideas and the actions you can commit to in a plan.

- **Share your plan with trusted advisors.** Choose people you trust and respect who will advise, encourage, and hold you accountable to your plan. Be very intentional with whom you share your dreams and make sure these are people who genuinely support you.

- **Track your progress.** Check off all the steps you've accomplished according to your plan and celebrate your progress, big or small. Tracking enables you to stay focused, measure your progress, and see your momentum (or where you're slacking).

Work for a Company That Also Works for You

Finding a company to work for is like finding a compatible life partner. Just as you have to make a wise choice on the person with whom you want to share your life, you must also choose wisely the employer to which you will devote a significant chunk of your time—one that will not only appreciate, leverage, and reward your talent, but will also sharpen your skills, increase your business acumen, hopefully allow you to learn from failure, and also build your human capital.

A company will be intentional about choosing you, so be intentional about choosing the company, too. The more thorough you are in your employment pursuits, the more likely you are to have a satisfying employment experience. Just be mindful there is no such thing as a perfect company because there are no such thing as perfect people.

When I made the pivot from one employer to another, the following three Ps guided me:

Principles

A company's guiding principles, what it stands for and believes, are its values. Values consistently modeled by leadership shape the organizational culture. People generally tend to have a better employment experience in environments where they fit and thrive in the culture. Values are not defined by words on a wall—that's marketing. Rather, company values are defined by behaviors and decisions executed by its leadership.

As you consider working for a company that also works for you, spend time with the employees of that organization and ask these questions:

- What is the culture like in this company?
- What do you like the most about working for this company?
- How are values recognized in this company? On your team?
- Which values get recognized and rewarded the most in the company?

People

While money and medical benefits are extremely important, there are other needs that must be met for us to engage in the workplace. As people, we have needs: to feel appreciated for the contributions we make, to be valued, to be seen and acknowledged, to grow, to be successful, and to feel safe.

When courting a company for potential employment opportunities, observe its employees. Do they appear happy and energized? Do they talk about how much they love the company they work for, even when they are off the clock?

Always do your research. When spending time with employees of that company, or during an interview, consider asking these questions:

- What is the company's retention rate?
- Why do employees leave?
- What is it about the company that keeps you engaged?

- How are growth and development encouraged in the organization? On your team?
- How does the company show grace if a goal or deadline isn't met?
- How often and in what ways is performance recognized?
- What does the career path look like for the role you are interviewing?
- Does the company offer tuition reimbursement or continuing education opportunities?
- How diverse is the C-suite?

Products

People generally find purpose and meaning working for an organization they believe in. They also need to have confidence in its products. When they do, they become more invested mentally, and perhaps even emotionally, in their work and take pride in it.

When looking for the right company, consider asking these questions of yourself:

- What brands are you a fan of?
- What brands do you follow on social media?
- Which iconic leaders do you follow? What brands, if any, do they endorse?
- Where do you spend a lot of your money?
- What companies have a loyal following of consumers?
- What kind of reputation does the company you are considering have?

Become Your Own Champion

Many people derive their sense of dignity and self-worth from their accomplishments on the job, which is why they often attach their value to titles and money. Be honest; during your annual review, have you ever asked the question, "What do I need to do to get promoted?"

This is not a bad question. In fact, it speaks to the heart of this book, to sojourn on a path that fuels our growth and our quest to self-maximize.

However, given the context of the question, there are two problems:

1. If you place your value in your company title or money, you are in trouble because you will feel lost and defeated if/when that goes away.

2. You're putting your trust in other people to tell you what you're worth and what you're capable of. In essence, you're deferring to other people to define and dictate your success for you rather than defining or creating it yourself. As a result, you might find yourself mimicking or conforming to other people rather than being true to your unique talent, personality, and identity. The truth is, you could check off every performance measure, work late nights, attend every dinner, travel to and live in every market, and still be overlooked for promotion.

In addition, there are those who believe that for you to advance in your career and have a seat at the table, you need a sponsor. Sponsors are company and institutional leaders with authority and influence who "adopt" you or have a personable relationship with you, advocate for you, and take a special interest in developing you and your career. Sponsors are always beneficial to have, but not everyone has a sponsor. Sponsors must see something in you and believe in you if they are going to put their name and reputation behind you.

But let's say nobody steps up to sponsor you, then what do you do? Or what if you feel isolated and alone because you're the only woman or other outlier on your team, and no one is on your side?

You must stand on your two feet and still believe in yourself no matter what, which is why you must have the mindset of being your own champion. When you grow yourself and obtain many wins on your own, the right sponsors will come.

Here is how I became my own champion:

- **Be responsible for your own success and development.** Change your mindset and remember that no one can walk your path but you. You must care about your own growth and success, and take the initiative. If you rely on a person, company, or system to feed you, you will always be dependent on them—and they will, in turn, have power and control over you.

- **Seek a mentor rather than a sponsor.** Find a mentor either inside or outside the company you work for to challenge your perspective, learn best practices, and glean wisdom.

- **Pursue interests outside your company.** Want to fuel your passion, develop your gifts, feed your curiosity, or grow your leadership? Go back to school. Take an online training course. Start your side hustle. Look for opportunities to serve or volunteer. You will fuel your momentum, increase your value, and gain a new sense of fulfillment outside the company.

- **Take risks.** Take advantage of opportunities that push you outside of your comfort zone. Every risk taken leads to a deeper revelation of your truest self, even if the risk itself leads to an unpleasant result. Like taking a test, you must expose yourself to challenges and opportunities to get to the bottom of how much you really know, where you naturally excel and fall short, and who and what you truly believe and value. This is how you grow in your personal power and become clear about how you see yourself and your role in this world. Taking risks also helps build your self-confidence and self-awareness.

Broaden Your Exposure

There is a world that exists outside of you. When we take an opportunity to listen and learn from others who are different from us, we grow. We grow in our compassion for humanity and empathy. Sometimes we become grateful, and hopefully more purposeful. Our consciousness evolves. We can challenge our assumptions of people, confront our conscious and unconscious biases, and broaden our worldview.

Here are ways I've broadened my exposure:

- **Travel.** Venture to a world that's different from your own. If you cannot have an international travel experience, consider engaging with different organizations and cultures within your immediate locale.

- **Listen and talk to people.** Have conversations with people at your company who are different from you. Learn their stories and be vulnerable in sharing yours.

- **Read books.** Especially read books by and about people whose experiences are different from yours.

Be Open to New Opportunities

Challenges stretch and shape you. You will not experience much growth sitting in the same seat, doing the same job, at your company forever. The experiences gained from new opportunities can sharpen your business acumen, expose you to influential leaders in your organization, hone your leadership skills, and increase your internal and external visibility and credibility.

However, it's important to differentiate a good opportunity from the *right* opportunity. Once you make the distinction, be intentional in saying no. Saying no to the good opportunities and yes to the right opportunities keeps you focused and protects your boundaries.

The following questions guide me when I consider new opportunities:

- **Does the opportunity align with my vision and goals?** Stay true to your path. If the opportunity falls outside the boundaries of what's important to you, turn it down.

- **Will my strengths or gifts be utilized in the opportunity?** Any opportunity that doesn't employ your strengths or natural abilities will not sustain you for long.

- **What is the ultimate value to me? How will I benefit from this opportunity?** Are the benefits worth it to you? What will you have to give up?

Remember Your Gift

Your gift is the biggest opportunity you own. It attracts other opportunities, makes you valuable and a standout, and it is where you will find success, prosperity, and personal fulfillment.

Activating your gift fuels your self-maximization, and it connects you to your purpose.

What uniquely comes to mind when people think of you? A great encourager of people? An excellent communicator? A moving vocalist? A formidable activist? A talented athlete? A captivating orator? If nothing *superlative* comes to mind when people think of you, that is a problem, because it means you're not known and regarded for anything special.

Your gift is inherent, but it must still be developed and refined with diligence before it is ripe and ready to share with the world (and you get paid for it). No company can fire your gift. Your gift will survive a crisis and outlast any pandemic. However, only you can activate it and determine what to do with it.

Some people know the gifts they possess while others do not. For me, I rediscovered and confirmed my gifts in the following ways:

- **Seek your Source.** If you are a person of faith, connect with your Source. Search yourself, reflect, meditate, pray, and listen to what your spirit is telling you.

- **Go back to the days of your youth.** As children, we lived out our imaginations. What do you remember doing for fun as a child? Who did you want to be when you grew up? What seemed to click for you?

- **Reflect upon what feels natural to you.** What type of work or activity feels like a natural extension of who you are? What work or activity gives you energy and makes you feel strong? If money weren't an issue, what might you dream of doing?

- **Think about what you are known for.** What do others say you do well? What does your team or your leader repeatedly select you, or favor you, to do? What physical, mental, or spiritual qualities do you possess that people admire?

- **Identify what makes you angry.** Your gift is not only meant to serve others, but it is also meant to solve a problem. What you often complain about could indicate your gift.

- **Pursue additional opportunities at your job.** Take advantage of opportunities that stretch you. Learn what you like and don't like. If you discover you have a particular knack or curiosity for something, follow it.

- **Serve.** Volunteer your time in a ministry, non-profit, or other service organization that you care about. Which committees or groups do you naturally gravitate to and are a natural fit?

- **Consider your environment.** Gifts are often stifled, caged, or buried in toxic, non-productive environments. Just like seeds need to be in the right environment to sprout, you need to be in the right space for your gift to be encouraged, nurtured, and developed.

- **Know your specialty.** There is something you can do that nobody else can, at least not quite like you. There's a unique quality you possess that affects others, breathes life, and adds value. What is it?

Prepare for the Pivot

Preparation is a major key to smooth transitions. Whether you choose to apply for another job within a company, apply to a different company altogether, or just simply make the pivot from a company to start your own business, you would be wise to set yourself up to win—especially if you have family responsibilities.

These are steps I took to prepare for my pivot out of corporate America:

- **Believe in yourself and in your value.** This is the hardest step. You must overcome your own self-doubt and believe you are capable, enough, and worthy of something better than what you have.

- **Do *not* make an emotional decision.** Are you offended at the office? Well, people come and people go; it's more important that you love your work. Don't get into your feelings when making an important career shift, and make sure *you* are not the problem, either. Do you currently have a good opportunity? Are you growing? Are you utilizing your gifts? Is there a viable career path ahead of you? Think it through. If you don't have absolute peace about leaving your employer, then stay. Maximize every opportunity you can from your company first before you take the leap.

- **Create a vision board.** What do you want to be known for? What does success look like for you? Put your purpose into pictures and post them on a board. This is so you can remind yourself of where you're headed and encourage yourself that the best is yet to come.

- **Develop a plan but set small goals at a time.** The vision board is the big picture, but your plan should also include small goals and daily habits, ones that will move you toward your desired future. Small wins lead to big gains. Set small goals that you know you can attain first, as this will fuel your momentum and motivation to set even bigger goals later. This step is imperative for individuals wanting to make the pivot from a company to becoming their own boss.

- **Work toward your vision/dream after you get home from the office.** If your desire is to start a business, keep your day job if necessary. Focus on completing at least one action item a day to develop your business. There is always something you can do. It doesn't matter how small the action is, just maintain a daily habit of working toward your vision or dream so that you're always moving. Momentum requires movement!

- **Get the training, certification, development, and/or experience you need (or enough of it) prior to your pivot.** Before you transition from one role or job to another, make sure you maximize every opportunity afforded to you in your existing role to set you up for success. If you plan to start your own business, utilize every resource that your company will pay for to develop and credential you, if possible.

- **Obtain best practices from other people who made career pivots to pursue their dream.** Learn from the experiences of individuals who have walked the path you'd like to take. There are many people who have taken risks to pursue their dream who can offer advice, stories, encouragement, and hopefully, connections.

- **Have seed money set aside.** If your goal is to exit your company to start your own business, it would be wise to have money set aside for start-up and personal living expenses. Yes, you can always take out a business loan, if approved, but having your own money stashed aside provides extra peace of mind. Saving money requires discipline, so be ready to make sacrifices for the sake of your goals.

- **Have a few paying opportunities before you leave your company.** This is so you have some level of revenue coming in once you transition fully into your own business.

- **Don't leave alone.** If you decide to make the pivot, have a team or community in place to help you—for example, someone who understands your industry, someone who understands accounting, another who knows legal concepts, and/or someone who is skilled in marketing. These can be your friends, mentors, partners, or paid professionals. They should believe in you and your vision, encourage you, and provide a measure of accountability to your goals. Make sure you trust them.

Grieve, Then Grow

One way to describe grief is the loss of a dream. It's in our nature to attach ourselves to anything significant and meaningful to us—not just a human relationship—like our goals, our aspirations, our ideals, our financial assets, our business, our titles, or our belief system.

When you work hard for something and/or someone, when you pour your soul and attach yourself into that dream you seek to manifest, it is a deep hurt when that dream is not realized, or it is attained, then later lost. That feeling of loss can lead to bitterness, anger, or in some cases, depression. For people who endured and survived a level of trauma at their companies—for example, toxic cultures, microaggressions, biases, non-supportive environments—there are usually side effects: feelings like shame, post-traumatic stress, a falling from grace, rejection, or even rage.

While many people are not inclined to discuss their grief, the only way out of the grieving period is to go through it. Emotional and psychological wounds cut deep and don't easily disappear, especially if you've been told repeatedly by someone in authority that you don't have what it takes.

The truth is, dealing with grief is a process that takes time. The good news is that successfully coping with grief leads to more maturity, more self-awareness, more wisdom and understanding, and more resilience.

The following steps helped me deal with grief after I made my pivot from corporate America:

- **Accept responsibility.** It takes two for any relationship or partnership to succeed or fail. To shift blame is to avoid looking within yourself to discover and deal with your own shortcomings. Own your mistakes.

- **Forgive.** Accept that what happened to you in your career took place. Learn and grow from the experience without allowing it to compromise your character. Let it go, move on, and don't look back. There is enough opportunity in this world for everybody.

- **Seek counseling.** It's unhealthy to keep negative emotions bottled up inside you. A trained professional can skillfully guide you through your different stages of grief.

- **Journal.** Another way to release your emotions is to write them in a journal. Consistent journaling tracks your progress, as well as your mental and emotional development. It forces you to think and reflect.

- **Exercise.** Go for a walk, lift weights, play a sport. Exercising lifts your mood and relieves stress. And looking better on the outside always helps.

Keep Growing

The real work—the most important job we have—is to become ourselves. Self-discovery takes time and is a process, with every experience, training, environment, relationship, success, and adversity peeling back the layers of our human existence to expose our truest nature. Self-maximization requires us to continually work at becoming the highest expression of ourselves, to own our opportunities, in every aspect of our lives. As long as we have breath, it is never too late to grow and maximize our individual humanity.

ACKNOWLEDGMENTS

Writing this book was one of the most painful projects I have ever undertaken. I am exceedingly grateful for my village that pushed me, encouraged me, and covered me with love and prayers from the beginning to the end: Michelle Gipson, my first editor, who held my hand and helped me to become a better writer; my mom, who has always been supportive of my writing and available to critique it; my dad and Joann for their cheers and encouragement; my sister, Alicia, and Antoine for listening to my readings even while at work or in the late hours; my cousins, Jennifer and Chase, who never stopped reminding me that "the people want NOW!"; my Uncle Sonny and Aunt Loretta, who always checked in on my progress and boosted my spirits; my sages and role models, Lisa Churchfield, Lana Porter, Martha P. Farmer and Patricia Russell-McCloud, who took me under their wing and strengthened me with their wisdom; my spiritual motivator, Coach Ken Coggins, who exhorted me to approach every day as "4th and inches" and to always keep the fire burning; my dear friend, Lolita, who reminded me that God wouldn't bring me this far to leave me hanging; and finally, my agent, Paul Levine, and editor, Debby Englander, for saying yes when everyone else said no.

ABOUT THE AUTHOR

Juliet Hall is the principal of Juliet Hall INC, a boutique leadership consulting agency based in Atlanta, Georgia. Recognized by several organizations in Atlanta as a "Top Black Woman of Influence," Juliet serves as an advisor and executive coach to C-suite and deputy leaders and speaks on national stages on the topics of servant leadership and self-maximization. She is passionate about helping leaders, especially women, who are at a professional crossroads to pursue their own self-discovery, develop their natural talents, and thrive in what they are uniquely created to do. With a professional background that includes twenty years of leadership in multi-billion dollar corporations, Juliet has presented her work to executives in government, education, healthcare, ministry, business, and non-profit. She is a member of Alpha Kappa Alpha Sorority, Incorporated and The Links, Incorporated. A graduate of Spelman College and the Terry College of Business at the University of Georgia, Juliet has traveled to over twenty countries and enjoys cardio boxing and playing tennis.